JUST EVERY DAY

Journal of a Mother's Grief

Pat McGrath

iUniverse, Inc.
New York   Bloomington

JUST EVERY DAY
Journal of a Mother's Grief

iUniverse books may be ordered through booksellers or by contacting:

iUniverse
1663 Liberty Drive
Bloomington, IN 47403
www.iuniverse.com
1-800-Authors (1-800-288-4677)

Because of the dynamic nature of the Internet, any Web addresses or links contained in this book may have changed since publication and may no longer be valid. The views expressed in this work are solely those of the author and do not necessarily reflect the views of the publisher, and the publisher hereby disclaims any responsibility for them.

ISBN: 978-1-4502-1980-8 (sc)
ISBN: 978-1-4502-1981-5 (ebook)

Printed in the United States of America

iUniverse rev. date: 4/21/2010

This book is dedicated to both the living and the dead. The latter refers to my son, Michael, who in many ways has made me who I am today. The former refers to my family and many friends, whose love and support have enabled me to continue.

I offer a very special dedication to Kenny and Julie. They, more than anyone, have stood by me through the trauma of the loss of my only child. They have been there for me in more ways than I can express. More importantly, I know they always will.

Contents

Introduction

I feel compelled to state at the outset that I am writing this primarily for myself. I apologize if this sounds self-serving, but I have learned through this process of grief that being self-absorbed at times is essential to regaining yourself. I am still very much within the throes of grief. I guess that's no surprise, considering that I am just now beginning my second full calendar year without my son. As I begin this writing, he died twenty-one months ago. The process of grief involved with his loss has been an up-and-down climb with unexpected turns and slippery conditions. However, there is one thing I know for sure: **it lasts forever.**

Writing has been a major part of the process for me. I find it healing to put my thoughts and feelings out there. The tears flow with the words, releasing the pressure that such emotion can cause. Therefore, the idea of writing initially came from my need to begin to heal. If anyone who happens to read these words finds consolation, I am grateful. If not, I have still accomplished my intended goal; the process of writing itself has moved me closer to the person I will become.

Grief changes you. It has changed me. I am a different person than I was before my son died. I am becoming a woman who at times is strange to me, but one whom I know will be better than the one I left behind. My son Michael changed me while he was alive, so I guess it is no surprise that his death should do the same. Sometimes I'm just amazed at the impact that one small, helpless life can have.

I knew when I first held him in my arms that my life would never be the same, but I had no idea just how true those words would be. I knew my time would no longer be my own. I was a single woman who had adopted a hard-to-place infant, so of course life would change for me. From the moment I first held him, the love I felt was like no other. I knew without a doubt that I would make whatever sacrifice was necessary to protect him; his needs would come first without question or regret. Suddenly, this small life was more valuable than my own. I am not at all sure how this happens, but I can say with certainty that the bond between a mother and her child is stronger than any I have experienced and, as such, that bond is never broken, not even by death.

1
Where It All Began

Biology is the least of what makes someone a mother.
—Oprah Winfrey

Let's start at the beginning. As a young, single adult, I thought about adopting a child many times, but something always interfered. The truth is that I was just not ready. In the early 1970s, I began to consider the idea once again. I was a single woman with a secure and rewarding career, but something was definitely missing from my life. Marriage did not seem to be anywhere on the horizon, but my desire to be a parent simply would not go away. I yearned to be a mother, and as I passed the age of thirty, thoughts of having a baby seemed to rule my mind.

At the time, I was living with friends who were married to each other and had three children of their own. We lived in a kind of Christian community, sharing resources and providing each other with support. The companionship was good for me, and I loved both of them and their children with all my heart. Still, I was restless. Helping to parent other people's children is not the same as having your own. I began to give serious thought to adopting a baby. The closer I got to a final decision, the more frightening the idea seemed to me, and I continued to find reasons to delay. Finally, I decided to go to graduate school first, thinking that such a degree would make my career even more secure.

I graduated in 1976 at the age of thirty-one with a Master's Degree in Counseling Psychology. Once school was finished, I took a much-needed vacation. At this point, the thought of adopting had not really been part of my conscious mind for quite some time. Then, the miracle happened! My first night home after my trip, I awoke suddenly; the digital clock read 4:00 am. I abruptly sat up in bed and heard myself say, "I'm going to adopt a baby." There was no fear that accompanied this announcement, just a realization that it would happen and my life would never be the same. I just knew that God wanted me to pursue this direction, although I had absolutely no idea when or how this miracle would occur. Later that morning, I told the other adults in my household that I was going to adopt a baby. We had discussed the possibility years before, and while they were not surprised at my announcement, the suddenness seemed to startle them. I went to work and continued with all the normal aspects of my life.

The process of single-parent adoption is certainly not easy, but I moved forward as best I could and followed every lead that came my way. Over the next several months, I pursued two individual ideas in particular. One possibility was to adopt a child through the Department of Immigration, and the other was to follow through on a lead provided by a good friend who worked in the field of human services. Everyone I knew who had ever adopted encouraged me to follow every possibility and not tell the left hand what the right hand was doing. They cautioned that when one agency knows you are also pursuing other avenues, you move down its list. So, I continued with both leads, confident that the right one would result in a successful adoption.

Life was quite hectic during this time. Adoption is so uncertain. When you are pregnant, you know for sure that something will occur within a definite time frame. Adoption is a day-to-day adventure. You never know if or when you will first hold your child in your arms. The time frame can be months, years, or never, so you just keep following through with all leads, praying one will result in a child soon. I did know that if a baby became available to me, it would not be a "healthy Caucasian infant." Single-parent adoption was unusual at that time, and generally only "hard to place" children found their way into such homes. I never understood the rationale behind this reality. If a two-parent family is *always* better for a "healthy Caucasian" infant, why is that less true for a child who doesn't fit into that category? I guess the truth is that children of color or those who are born with various health conditions are better off with a single parent than no parent at all. As sad as that is, it really didn't matter to me if I received a child who was neither healthy nor white. I believed that I was meant to pursue this adoption, and I had faith that I would find the resources to raise my child to be a happy and productive adult.

In spite of my openness to a wide variety of options, I was also aware that this decision would affect more than just me. As such, I felt it was important that I let my parents know I was pursuing a somewhat unconventional adoption. I went to their home one evening after work and told them my plans. I was quick to inform them that this child would very likely be biracial. My father immediately got teary-eyed as he listened to my description. When I asked him what was wrong, he simply said, "Did you think we would care?" He was actually offended that I feared the race of their first grandchild would matter to them. I don't think I ever loved my father more than I did at that moment. From that day on, both my parents wholeheartedly supported my efforts to adopt a child and bring him or her into our family.

2
Miracles Do Happen

The most wonderful thing about miracles
is that they sometimes happen.

—G. K. Chesterton

In January 1977, my world changed forever. Things were moving very fast now. It seemed that both agencies were seriously considering me as an adoptive parent. A home visit by a state-sponsored social worker was scheduled for January 6 of that year. The process was grueling. The social worker arrived at our home at eight o'clock in the morning, and the interviews lasted a little over seven hours. She had asked that we keep the kids home from school for the morning because she wanted to interview them as well. We had prepared the kids as best we could, but I had no idea what they would say. They were just young children, ages ten, six, and four. I later found out that the six year old told the social worker that the only thing she was worried about was that the baby would look like a "zebra." Apparently, the image of a zebra was in her mind because we had talked about the baby possibly being biracial, both black and white! The memory of this still brings a smile to my face. It never occurred to me how an innocent young child would grapple with the concept of a baby that was both "black and white." Obviously, at the age of six she had no frame of reference for this information, so she created one of her own, and quite a reasonable one, I might add. In her young mind, a baby was a baby, something to love, to hold, and to play with. But a baby who looked like a "zebra"? She wasn't so sure about that! The lesson taught by that little six-year-old girl was not lost on me.

The social worker interviewed us individually and together throughout the day; absolutely every aspect of my life was discussed and dissected. I knew this part of the process was essential to being approved as a parent, but I also knew I could not control the outcome, so I prayed. With almost every question, I had to make a decision as to just how honest I would be. For example, several years earlier, my twenty-nine-year-old sister Susan had died from complications caused by alcoholism. When asked about my family of origin, I debated as to how truthful I should be. Did the interviewer believe that alcoholism was somehow genetic, making it a liability in my case? I had no way of knowing what was in her mind, so I made a decision to be as truthful as I could and leave the results in God's hands. It was a truly humbling experience.

The interviewer was very good at her job; I never could get even a sense of how I was doing. Finally, she said she had enough material and would prepare her report. I walked her to the door, hoping to find out anything about her decision and finally, after seven hours, she rewarded me with a smile. She told me that upon her arrival she was very skeptical because I was single, and she was sure that at best she would approve me to adopt a little girl. However, she was so impressed with our "family" that she now knew her report would include an unconditional approval. I could have hugged her on the spot. What a relief!

Six days later, I was driving home from work with my mind in turmoil. At that time in my career, I was working four nights a week as a family counselor, and my shift ended at 10:00 pm. That night, the weather was dreadful—it was sleeting and I could barely keep the ice off my windshield. I just remember feeling terrified, not so much about the weather, but because I had received two separate telephone calls that day and both adoption agencies were moving toward fruition at breakneck speed. I was so scared. I knew I could not manage two babies, but I didn't know how I would choose. I was crying hard in the car, begging

God to send me a sign telling me what direction I should take. I made it painfully clear to Him that I needed a definite sign. I needed one of those tree-falling-in-the-road kind of signs; nothing vague would do. We were talking about two helpless babies here, and I had to know for sure. I arrived home safely and went straight to bed.

At seven o'clock the next morning, the phone rang. It was my lawyer with the announcement that my child had been born. It was a baby boy, born at ten fifteen the night before. I almost dropped the phone; my son had been born at exactly the moment I was screaming at God to send me a sign. I knew right then that the tree had indeed fallen across the road. This boy was meant to be my son, and I never doubted that fact from that moment on.

Despite everything, I was not prepared for his arrival. I knew too well that adoption can take a long time, and it had only been seven months since I first applied. I was determined not to set myself up for repeated emotional letdowns by having everything ready for a baby who may never arrive. So when the call came so quickly, I had nothing prepared. There was no adorable nursery and no dresser full of darling outfits. So much had to be done, and it had to be done quickly.

I started with the nursery. Friends chipped in and we created a perfect space for a newborn boy. We added a fresh coat of paint to the walls before we hung all the darling animal decals. There was a giraffe, cuddly bears, little monkeys, and an elephant now on the walls. We assembled the crib with a playful mobile hanging overhead; the changing table and dresser were in place. I ran from store to store, purchasing diapers, undershirts, booties, and one-piece outfits; crib sheets and blankets, washcloths and bath towels to wrap around him; sweaters and a yellow snowsuit in which to bring him home. The excitement was overwhelming. I could hardly remember to breathe. I was about to have a baby, and the thrill of it all brought me more joy than I could have ever imagined.

Four days later, I was scheduled to be in court to secure the adoption. My family was thrilled and anxiously awaiting my return. My parents were at my home ready to welcome their first grandchild. The nursery was finished and all the necessary baby things had been purchased. I was ready to be a mom.

I arrived at the office of the Department of Children and Family Services. This was to be my first stop. The birth mother was scheduled to arrive there as well, but at a different time. The process had been well defined for both of us. I remember sitting alone in a small gray cubicle across from a rather matronly-looking social worker. She had my file in front of her and kept shaking her head and saying, "This is highly unusual" over and over again. I felt doomed. How could I convince her that this "unusual" adoption was meant to be? Finally, she announced that she had to consult her supervisor and left the cubicle. I was terrified that I would be caught in the midst of some bureaucratic snag that was totally beyond my control. I waited for what seemed like forever. Unbeknownst to me, the home study report was not yet part of the file. The interview had only occurred a few days before, and the agency had not yet received the report. When the social worker returned to the cubicle, she looked like a different person. With a big smile on her face, she announced that everything was in order, offered her congratulations, and directed me to the courthouse to complete the adoption procedure. I later discovered that the mail had arrived while I was waiting and the home study report, with its unconditional approval, had been received. The miracles just kept coming!

I headed for the courthouse, feeling like I could have walked on air. However, once I saw my attorney, I knew by the look on his face that something was terribly wrong. All he said was, "She wouldn't sign the papers." I knew this meant that, at the last possible moment, my child's birth mother had changed her mind. He went on to tell me that, after being released from the hospital, the young girl had taken off and no one knew her whereabouts. The birth mother was a scared eighteen-year-old girl who had no support from her parents and was facing this ordeal alone. Nonetheless, I was devastated. I had to return home without my baby.

All I could think about on the way home was how scared and conflicted she must be. This young girl was just a teenager, and she had to make one of the most important decisions of her young life all by herself. No wonder she was scared. It was also easy to understand why she felt so conflicted. How could you not when you're asked to relinquish all rights to your child? I told my lawyer not to contact me again until all the necessary legal papers were signed. I returned home and began the agonizing process of waiting hour after hour for the phone to ring. Nothing further happened that day, and I announced to everyone that we should return to our normal lives. We all went back to work, and my parents went home to await my call. These were some of the longest days in my life. I had done all I could; it was totally out of my hands. All I could do was pray and wait.

Late in the evening of January 18, my attorney called to inform me that I was to be in court at 11:00 am the next morning to complete the process before going to the hospital to pick up my son. I could hardly believe my ears. It was really going to happen. I was going to be a mother. I silently said a prayer of thanksgiving, asking the Lord to bless the young girl whose child I was about to receive.

I went to court the next morning and adopted my son. Once all the legal requirements were properly met, I was driven by friends to the hospital to pick up Michael and bring him home. I remember looking through the nursery window at the hospital, trying to pick out which baby was Michael. Quickly I realized that he was the one who looked different from all the others. Every infant was wrapped in either a pink or a blue blanket, except one. That tiny little child was covered in a soft green wrap. I guess it was suppose to signify that this child did not yet have a name or proud parents to claim him. The staff needed to set him apart. I remember telling Michael this story many years later. Unfortunately, it only seemed to reinforce in his mind that he was different, and to him, "different" was a bad thing to be. I preferred to think of "green" as the Irish do, bringing good luck, for I knew in my heart that I was lucky to be bringing this child into my life, and I prayed that he would one day feel lucky too.

The early years seemed difficult at the time, but as it turned out, they were a breeze compared to what followed. I can still remember how it felt to hold him in my arms and just study his face. He was such a beautiful baby. Back in the 1970s, adoptive mothers didn't get maternity leave, so I had to go back to work after a two week "vacation." Michael was three weeks old, and I remember how hard it was to leave him. I so enjoyed the early morning feeding when I was alone with him in the quiet of a sleeping house. I guess I was young enough that the lack of sleep was not a concern for me. I was blessed that my mother was initially available to watch him while I worked. So for the first eight months, I brought him to my mom's house each morning. This involved carting most of his gear, because all my mom had was a crib and a highchair. I really did not mind though, because I knew he was lovingly cared for, and it gave me the opportunity to be with him each night.

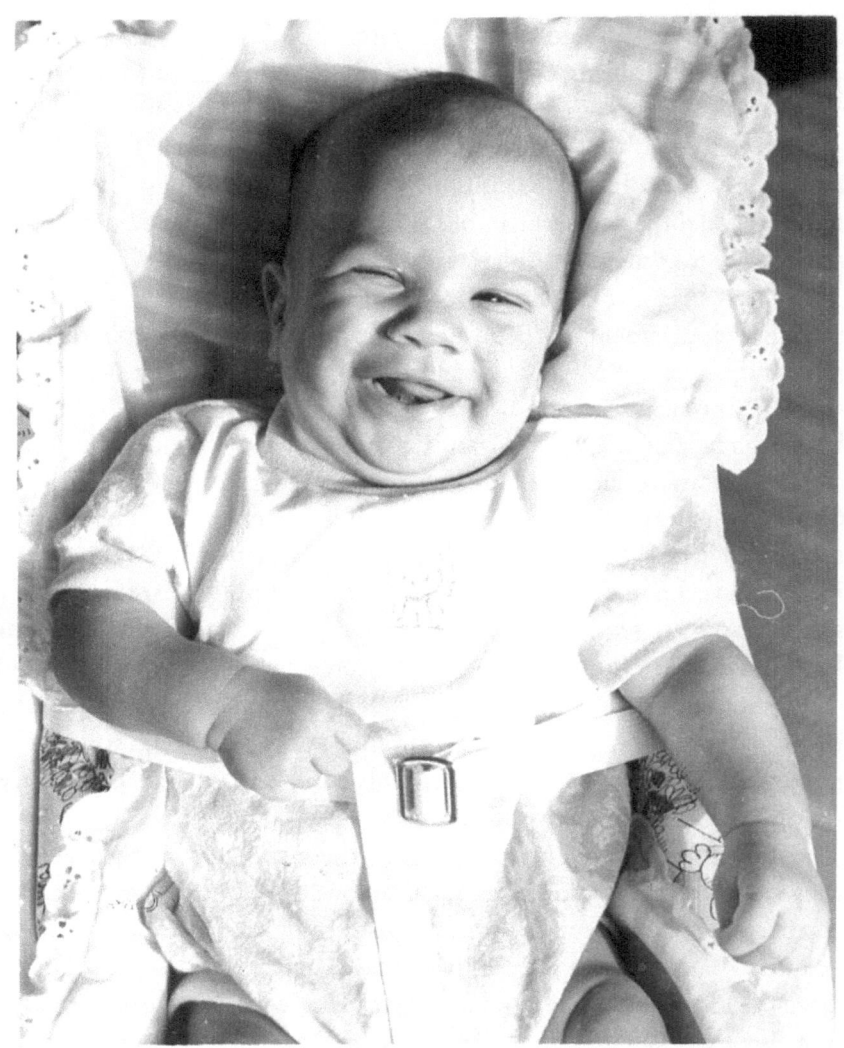

Michael's winning smile!

Things changed rapidly after those first eight months. In addition to caring for Michael, my mother was struggling to care for three terminally ill adult family members, one of whom was my father. It was painfully apparent to me that it was just too much for her. Therefore, I began the frightening process of looking for affordable, quality childcare. Within a few months, my father died of cancer, just nine days after Michael's first birthday. Though I was saddened by the loss, I was grateful that my dad had some time to enjoy his only grandchild. It was obvious that the baby brought a measure of joy to my father's life, and I hope that joy eased his pain in those final days.

At some point during this time, I realized that my son was going to be more than the usual challenge. Early on, I described him to others as "unconfineable." He managed to get himself out of virtually every kind of device manufactured to keep babies safe. He would watch me put up the sides of his playpen, and the minute I turned around, he would flip the hinges, let the sides down, and crawl away. I had two separate seat belts for his car seat, yet one day while driving, I looked in my rearview mirror to see him lying under the back window making faces at the people in the car behind us. Before he could walk, he learned to flip himself over the top of his crib and scoot around his room to discover whatever he could. A friend suggested I put a top on his crib, and at first, I agreed. However, the sight of such a contraption brought me to tears, and I removed it immediately. Instead, I scoured his room each night, making sure there was nothing he could get into that would be dangerous to him.

As he grew, he quickly mastered the doorknob, and his wandering expanded to the whole house. On the advice of his pediatrician, I reversed the knob of his bedroom door and locked him in his room each night to keep him safe. One night, when he was not yet three years old, I woke around 2:00 am to the sound of him singing "Itsy Bitsy Spider" outside my bedroom window. He had pushed out the screen, crawled out his bedroom window, and was wandering around our suburban yard. I was terrified that he would wander off during the night. From that point on I also secured his bedroom window to prevent him from injury. I couldn't find a single book that offered direction for raising a child like Michael. I felt like I was in it alone, and I knew that I had absolutely no idea how to successfully raise him. Instinct and faith in God were all I had, and I learned to rely on them completely.

Michael was very bright, and his intelligence partly fueled his curiosity. I can still see him sitting on the family room floor on a warm summer day. He was around eighteen months old and had discovered a large black flashlight on the table. He studied the object and for several minutes meticulously took it apart, placing each small item on the floor next to him. Unlike what one might expect, he never tried to put any of the pieces in his mouth. Rather, he lined them up in the same order with which he had removed them. A friend of mine was also in the room, and he and I were spellbound while we watched this small child sit quietly and reassemble the flashlight piece by piece. I knew at that moment that my son was truly exceptional; I just had no idea in what positive and negative directions his talents would take him.

3
Scared and Confused

Courage is resistance to fear, mastery of fear—not absence of fear.

—Mark Twain

The stress related to raising Michael grew each day until finally, when he was almost three, I accepted the advice of his pediatrician and took him to a nearby children's hospital for a complete neurological evaluation. The appointment was with the head of the department of child neurology. I recognized his name from some of the many articles I had read in my effort to better understand what Michael needed. He was identified as a noted expert in the field of child neurology. Surely, this renowned physician would be able to help.

I can still see the technician trying to administer the EEG. Michael was fidgety and full of questions, and she was trying hard to respond as one might to a normal three year old. Michael just kept screaming and pulling the apparatus off his head. I calmly tried to encourage the technician to just answer his questions fully. Finally, she told him that the device was made of "little cameras" that were going to take pictures of his head. This did not appease him, and he yelled that she was lying because he knew that wires had electricity and they would send the "lectricity" into his brain. Needless to say, when the EEG was finally administered, it came back as significantly abnormal with multiple spiked areas. Later, the child neurologist examined him and reviewed the test results. He then called me into his office. He told me that Michael likely was hydrocephalic, a serious medical condition describing an excess of fluid in the brain. The doctor wanted to schedule more perceptual tests to make sure. I cried all the way home that afternoon because I was terrified of what such a diagnosis could mean.

We returned for further testing two weeks later, and Michael scored off the intellectual charts. In particular, his verbal skills were remarkable. At this point, the renowned child neurologist told me, "If he was hydrocephalic, it was arrested," and prescribed a daily dose of Dilantin. He wanted me to return with Michael in six months. I was not comfortable with the idea of medicating such a young child, especially when the diagnosis was so uncertain. Therefore, I chose to get a second opinion. The second child neurologist disagreed with the diagnosis of hydrocephalus and told me that all Michael needed was more consistency in parenting. While I was also uncertain about this diagnosis, it was much easier to take than the previous direction. In addition, I thought that perhaps he was right. After all, there were three adults in our household, all providing direction and support to this child. Perhaps he really was confused, and a more consistent approach was the answer.

My friends and I discussed the issue and committed to a much more consistent approach in parenting this small child. For several months, our home took on the appearance of an army boot camp. We all consistently responded to Michael's behavior in exactly the same manner, but despite our efforts, his behavior didn't changed. I was becoming more confused every day.

Finally, I had had enough. With the help of my pediatrician, I made an appointment for Michael at the Mayo Clinic in Rochester, Minnesota. I knew something was terribly wrong. I figured if anyone could tell me what it was, it would be the specialists at such a renowned medical facility. Michael was put through numerous neurological and psychological tests, and the rest of us were interviewed many times as well. The entire process took several days, but we ended up going home with no more answers than we had when we arrived. The doctors all agreed that there were definite neurological signs of concern, but because of his young age, they were unable to provide me with a clear sense of medical direction. They advised that we keep doing what we were doing and bring Michael back in a few years when his brain and neurological system were more definitively developed.

In the end, after seeing many specialists and taking many tests, I could not find two doctors who agreed on what was wrong with my son. To make matters worse, their opinions varied greatly. This is the point at which my confusion over his medical condition began. That confusion grew even more complex as I consulted more experts, looking for a definitive answer. The final answer was that there was no real answer.

It was many years and many doctors later that I learned that Michael suffered from a kind of brain damage probably due to the drugs his birth mother took early in her pregnancy. The adoption agency never provided any of that information, and I prefer to believe that they did not know at the time. Michael's mother was an eighteen-year-old high school student from a neighboring county. She worked part-time at a local fast food restaurant and had no help from her parents. The maternal grandparents would not provide any assistance because they were afraid their daughter would choose to keep her baby and they refused to have a "black" grandchild. The father was in the armed services and out of state by the time Michael was born. Michael's birth mother was several months along by the time she sought assistance from a local clinic. Once a part of the program, she did well with the prenatal care and counseling they provided. This young girl struggled alone through a very difficult time in her life and had a very hard time giving up her baby. I bear her no ill will, but I wish she had provided more information about her early drug use. I would have adopted Michael no matter what, but perhaps I could have helped him better and sooner had I known more. To this day, I thank God for the gift that young girl provided. I never regretted adopting Michael, and I never will.

School was probably the most difficult aspect of Michael's life. It wasn't because he was slow; quite the contrary. He was very bright, and much of the academic part of school came easily to him. Rather, his problems were all behavioral. I was asked to remove him from three preschools before he was four years old. My local school district tested him and found that he was intellectually gifted. They encouraged me to admit him into school early, and after careful thought, I agreed. Michael entered kindergarten at the age of four.

However, I knew from the very first day that problems would occur.

I remember walking him to the school for an orientation to kindergarten. The children went with the teacher, while the parents all met with the principal. When the orientation was over and we were walking home, I asked Michael how he liked his teacher. He looked up at me and simply responded, "She lies, mom." I asked what he meant, and he reported that the teacher told them that each Friday they would form a circle and she would stand in the middle, close her eyes and point to one of the children. The one she chose would then be able to take the Paddington Bear home for the weekend. She assured the class that everyone would get a turn. I asked him what was wrong with that idea. He said, "If she really had her eyes closed, we wouldn't all get a turn." I was stunned.

His language skills were developing rapidly. He had been reading for some time. His favorite bedtime reading was a large storybook of Greek mythology; sometimes I would read it to him and other times he would read to me. He knew the names of many of the Greek gods and could spell them correctly. These accomplishments did not really frighten me; rather they seemed normal for Michael. He had been speaking in sentences since before he walked, and I grew somewhat comfortable with his exceptional verbal skills.

Michael played the piano from the time he was a toddler. At first, he plucked out songs he seemed to hear in his head. As he grew, the complexity of his music grew with him, and he frequently amazed me with the sounds he created. He always seemed to be composing the music as he played, and it was truly beautiful.

Despite his intelligence and obvious musical talent, Michael had nothing but problems in school. I received calls from teachers and principals almost weekly, and no one seemed to have any answers. With the assistance of medical and educational personnel, I continued to search for direction on how to help my son. My own educational background provided me with enough information to know that there was something seriously wrong with Michael's ability to process information. From a very early age, no amount of consistent discipline had any effect on him at all. He would draw on the wall with crayon after he was told numerous times not to do it. I would give him a "time-out" and he would cry and promise never to do it again. After the time-out, he would often repeat the same behavior a few minutes later. It seemed as if his hand would draw before his brain received the message that he would get another time-out for it. This cyclical process repeated itself endlessly. Often I would go to bed at night feeling like a failure as a mother because all I had accomplished that day was to give Michael one punishment after another until it was time for him to go to bed.

In spite of the behavior problems that Michael routinely exhibited, I would not describe him as defiant. He clearly seemed as confused as I was by the fact that none of our attempts to manage his behavior worked. His remorse was always genuine, and I could see that the struggle was having a seriously negative impact on his self-esteem. Clearly, he was getting the message that something was wrong with him, that he was somehow "bad," and he had no idea how to improve the situation, no matter how much he wanted to please me and the other adults in his life. In retrospect, I cringe at how difficult this must have been for a four-year-old child to understand. No matter how hard he tried, he simply could not adapt to the limits of appropriate behavior, and in his mind, it was his fault.

4
Medication: Friend or Foe?

*It is our choices that show what we truly are
far more than our abilities.*
                                    —Joanne Kathleen Rowling

Early in 1982, Michael was finally diagnosed with Attention Deficit Hyperactivity Disorder (ADHD). The child psychiatrist involved encouraged me to put him on Ritalin, but I wanted to try less drastic methods of treatment due to his young age. We tried every possible alternative, but nothing seemed to work. Finally, Michael went through a period in which he did not sleep through the night for eight days in a row. He would doze for forty-five minutes to an hour, and then he would be up and moving. I was exhausted. Then I was giving him a bath one night and felt a gash on the top of his head. It was caked with dried blood, and it scared me to death. I had no recollection of him injuring himself and had to face the reality that it must have happened during the night while I was sleeping. I had no clear idea how it occurred or if it rendered him unconscious. I contacted the doctor and agreed to put him on Ritalin. I was terrified of the long-term effects of placing my five-year-old child on a controlled substance, but the alternatives seemed even worse.

I can still vividly recall his first day on a very low dose of Ritalin. I came home from work to find my extremely hyperactive child quietly sitting on the couch, reading a book. When I walked in, he looked up for a moment, said, "Hi Mom," and immediately went back to reading. This calm, normal greeting was so incredibly unlike the Michael I knew that I was stunned. I managed to say hi back before I nearly fell over. He was not running around in circles, jumping off furniture, yelling out how glad he was to see me. He was sitting and reading one of his many books. I honestly thought I had died and gone to heaven. I must say that of all the medical interventions that followed in the years ahead, Ritalin was really the only one that consistently helped my son.

Despite the medication, school continued to be a struggle for Michael. Most of his teachers did not have the time, energy, or skill to cope with a child with his needs. He was always in special education classes, and while this addressed some problems, it posed different concerns. For the most part, the classes were designed for children with various behavioral disorders. I always thought it odd that children who did not behave appropriately were placed in classes with others who had behavioral problems, thereby making it virtually impossible for them to learn acceptable behavior through the example of those around them. Some children with special needs are met with a caring and compassionate response from the adults around them. It is certainly not difficult for any of us to feel compassion for a sick or physically disabled child. However, that is not the response that children with emotional and/or behavior disabilities usually encounter. Unfortunately, many adults respond only to the behavior, not really seeing the child's struggle. Children want to please adults, and when they consistently do not, there is usually a reason, often beyond the obvious. Children with behavior disorders often receive only anger and frustration from the adults in their world. While in some ways this is understandable, in my opinion, it says more about us than the children involved. For example, Michael's problems were usually not met with a sympathetic response from the adults in his world because his behavior was so annoying and difficult to deal with. Rather, he was considered a "brat," an unruly child who needed to be disciplined for his inappropriate behavior. I remember so well struggling with this concept myself. I told the psychiatrist treating him at the time that I was having such a hard time disciplining him because the experts had told me that his behavior was a direct result of neurological disabilities. Would I force my child to get up and run a race when he was physically unable to do so? Of course not; no good parent would act in such a way. How then should I discipline my child who seemed incapable of behaving within the boundaries of normalcy that had been set for children without his problems? The psychiatrist eased my mind by telling me that I had to discipline him even when he was not capable of adhering to my guidelines, because that was the only way he would ever learn what appropriate behavior was and it was my role to teach him. He added that as long as I continued to separate my love for him from my disapproval of his actions, Michael was bright enough to eventually get the message. The psychiatrist told me to keep telling Michael how much I loved him no matter what he did, and though I knew it was difficult for him, he was capable of positive change.

I certainly understand that children with behavior problems pose significant and unique problems for teachers as well as classmates. However, in some ways it might be more beneficial for such children to learn appropriate behavior from kids in ordinary classes. I guess the truth is that there are no easy answers to such dilemmas. Yet I must say that I found very few teachers and/or educational administrators helpful. The vast majority seemed to have little understanding of Michael's problems and even less compassion for his struggle. While I understood that no one would ever love Michael as I did, I was saddened to encounter so many teachers, many of whom were in special education, who simply wanted him out of their rooms or their school.

In large part, this experience prompted me to run for election to my local school board. I knew firsthand the struggles of "special ed" kids and their parents and felt I had something unique to offer the district. Parents of "special" kids rarely attend school board meetings and voice their concerns. They are not like parents of student-athletes or gifted students. What parent of a gifted child is afraid to stand up and fight for a quality gifted program? What parent of a recognized athlete is hesitant to advocate for a state-of-the-art gymnasium? Such parents are proud of their children's accomplishments, and rightfully so. They want to do everything they can to increase the opportunity for their continued success. On the other had, parents of "special ed" kids often feel responsible for their children's struggle. Like all parents, they just want their children to fit in, be happy, and experience some measure of success as they proceed through school. I think this is even more true for parents whose children are in special education classes specifically because of behavior problems. How does a parent stand up in a crowd and fight for her "behavior disordered" child when she does not understand the problem, when she feels responsible for the problem, and when she has no idea how to help the child she loves so dearly?

I ran for the board largely on this platform and was elected. I served for several years and worked very hard to represent the needs of all of our kids, including those who were in special education. I can honestly say that I was not a one-issue board member, as I felt that would be unfair to the population at large. The other board members and the community soon recognized me as the one who would speak for kids who did not have a voice. I also made it a practice to keep my personal issues and my board responsibilities separate. Though some of the district administrators might disagree, I never used my position on the board to impact Michael's school experience. At one point, this became even more difficult because Michael's doctors were recommending that he be placed in a special school to address some of his problems. The school district was fighting this placement because the cost was significant. I never spoke to any of the other board members about this potential conflict. Given the fact that names were confidential, I did not want to have even the appearance of impropriety. At the same time, I did not want my son adversely impacted by the fact that I was on the school board. The only avenue to take was complete confidentiality. Despite my efforts, the board did discover the specifics of this disagreement because of an inappropriate communication by a district administrator. In addition, I was shocked to open the local newspaper and read of my son's struggle. Michael also read the article, and his reaction brought me to tears. He felt so ashamed knowing that the local kids in the neighborhood and at his school would now know more than they should about his problems. Clearly, my position on the school board was what made this a newsworthy story, and I was angry. This was a direct effort to sabotage my bid for re-election. These people were in positions designed to help children. How could they be so insensitive to the feelings of one small child? Well, their actions backfired. Like all the other candidates, I was invited to speak at a community forum prior to the election. I identified myself as the mother in the newspaper story, and I spoke honestly to the audience about the personal circumstances described in the article. I also spoke of my record as a board member and my vision for the district as a whole. Despite the unprofessional behavior of one district administrator, I was re-elected to my position on the board and served another two years. I am proud of my service to this board, and I hope that my knowledge and experience helped some youngsters who may have previously been invisible to those making decisions about their educational needs. If I helped even one child, it was worth my effort.

In the early years, Michael's intelligence exacerbated his problems in school. Most of the youngsters in his special classes were slower learners, and often his ability to grasp information quickly just added to his struggle. He was easily bored, and this led to even more behavioral problems. In one class, he was actually scolded because he knew too much, answered too quickly, and did not give others a chance to respond. His problems certainly went beyond simple boredom. From the very beginning, he seemed to rebel against most authority. If something didn't make sense to him, he fought it with seemingly boundless energy. For example, I remember one struggle that occurred when long division was introduced at school. He received a failing grade on a homework assignment in which he completed only four of the twelve problems. He had refused to go any further because he felt by completing the first four problems correctly he had demonstrated that he understood the concept and there was no point in finishing the rest of the assignment. He was ready to move on, and stubbornly refused to go along with the program.

There are hundreds of examples like that in my life with Michael. I tried repeatedly to teach him the value of "playing by the rules" whether or not they made sense to him. Sometimes he would go along, but mostly it was just to please me. More often, he stood his ground and suffered the consequences. As he got older, his bright mind became more of an asset and less of a liability. He started to use his brain to compensate for his disabilities, and this, coupled with an innate charm, helped him to experience some measure of success in school.

Michael continued to struggle through early childhood. His medication was increased as he developed physically and soon he was taking 80 mg of Ritalin a day at age eight. His problems at school also increased during this period and finally he was placed in a special school for children with a wide range of disabilities. The facility had a noted child neurologist on staff and he recommended additional medication to Michael's daily regimen. I was at a loss to deny such a request because I had no better ideas as to how to deal with his problems. He was in this school for almost two years, and by the end, Michael was taking 80 mg of Ritalin, 225 mg of Cylert, and 50 mg of Imipramine a day. He was nine years old and weighed seventy-one pounds. I was terrified of the potential impacts of such a medical regimen and sought out additional medical advice.

The physician I chose was a renowned child psychiatrist who came highly recommended by a number of credible sources. After one extensive interview with Michael and a review of his medical history, he was seriously alarmed at the amount of medication Michael took on a daily basis. He told me that I must get Michael off all medication, as the current regimen could well be doing him "irrevocable neurological damage." I was overwhelmed. One doctor recommends one course of action that another thinks is severely damaging to my son. It was at this point that I fully realized that the doctors had no answer either. In some ways, I knew as much about how to deal with Michael as the experts did, and I knew very little. I prayed for guidance and decided to take my son off all medication. He was not quite ten years old at the time.

I had to wean him off the drugs little by little, often cutting tiny pills in half for days at a time. The doctor in charge at this point had drafted a very detailed plan, and I followed it religiously. It took a total of six weeks over that summer to cleanse Michael's system of medication. During this time, his behavior became more extreme than I had ever witnessed before. I had to keep him within arms reach of a supervising adult at all times. He was virtually out of control. By the end of this period, it was evident that he needed to be hospitalized, and I admitted him into a child psychiatric hospital. This was the most difficult decision I had to make in our life together up to that point. Once again, I didn't know if I was doing the right thing, but at the time, I didn't see any other viable options. It turned out just to be the first of several hard decisions on the horizon.

He was in the hospital for six weeks, and I visited as often as they would allow. I stayed in close contact with the doctors, who tried a variety of medications and treatment modalities to assist Michael in regaining some measure of control over his impulsive behavior. None of the medications did any good at all, and eventually they prescribed Mellaril, an antipsychotic drug more commonly used in the treatment of schizophrenia. I was confused as to why the doctors were recommending it in Michael's case as it was not routinely used to treat Attention Deficit Hyperactivity Disorder. The doctors informed me that they believed Michael may be suffering from multiple conditions, possibly including psychotic disorders that were difficult to specifically diagnosis at his young age. The results of the Mellaril were devastating. Michael was at home during this period and did not attend school at all. Over a six-month span, his weight doubled from seventy pounds to almost one hundred and forty. He had an insatiable appetite and devoured everything in sight. It was as if he was blowing up like a balloon. In addition, he had minimal energy. He did nothing but eat and sleep. He was no longer a behavioral problem; he functioned like a zombie. I knew there had to be a better answer, so I informed the doctors that I wanted him off the Mellaril immediately, and they concurred.

Once again, when he was not medicated, the behavioral struggles reappeared. By this time, he was demonstrating symptoms of what the doctors feared might be Tourette's Syndrome. I remember being asked to attend a conference with the doctors. During this meeting, they informed me that it seemed we had only two choices left. We could put Michael back on lower doses of Ritalin, which would help his behavior but could accelerate the Tourette's if he had it, or we could continue to try to manage him without medication. The decision was mine to make, and they had no other alternatives. I knew in my heart that Michael could not survive in this world without medication. Experiments thus far with no medication had been disastrous.

I remember feeling both scared and angry in those days. The cause of my fear is obvious. The anger was initially directly at the doctors, the hospitals, and the experts upon whom I was supposed to be able to rely. How could they be so unsure, so unknowledgeable about the best way to help my son? How could they expect me to make such a decision? I was not an expert. That's when it dawned on me. Like it or not, I *was* in fact the expert. I was his mother and he was my son. The doctors were all telling me that they had no answers. The only place left to look was within myself. Michael was counting on me. I could not let him down, so I prayed to be able to make the right decision in spite of my fears.

Then I confidently opted to resume the Ritalin, which was the only drug that had ever helped at all without immediate and devastating side effects. The hospital made me sign a paper that I would not sue them if this proved to be the wrong decision. I signed because I knew it was the only reasonable option and that a loving God was there to help me care for this precious child.

5
Hard Choices

Life is not a continuum of pleasant choices,
but of inevitable problems that call for
strength, determination, and hard work.

—Indian proverb

Soon after Michael went back on the Ritalin, he was placed in an outpatient hospital educational program. This turned out to be a bad decision. The program was not designed for a child like Mike, and I removed him as soon as I could find a suitable alternative. At this point, all of the experts involved believed that Michael needed to be admitted into a residential treatment program. I found a professional woman who reviewed such programs nationally, and I hired her to find the best alternative for Michael. So in the fall of 1989, at the age of twelve, Michael was admitted to a residential treatment program in northern Ohio, a seven and a half hour drive from our home in Illinois. This decision proved to be even more difficult than the hospitalization, because I knew it would be for a longer period of time. Once again I felt like I was abandoning my child to the care of others, but I didn't know what else to do.

Initially, the placement seemed positive. Michael was doing well, and the respite that the placement provided me certainly was welcome. I spoke to him often on the phone and visited him one weekend every month. The other two adults in our household also visited regularly, and we all made a concerted effort to encourage Michael, assuring him that he would be welcome back home soon.

Michael's best picture, age twelve

As I mentioned earlier, I drove to Ohio one weekend every month to visit my son. Little by little, my concern with the placement began to grow. I was aware that various staff members were calling me more frequently between my visits. They were all aware that I had some academic credentials in the area of adolescent development, and they were calling with questions about how to handle specific problems they were encountering. At first, I was pleased with their calls, because they kept me well informed about Michael's status. However, as the frequency increased, I started to wonder about their level of competence.

In addition, my visits often resulted in a heightened sense of anxiety. I began to see serious signs that Michael was becoming institutionalized. Often during my visits, I would take him off campus for various outings. Sometimes we'd go shopping for clothes, have lunch out somewhere, or take in a movie that he wanted to see. One such Saturday, we were shopping, and I noticed that he kept checking his watch and telling me "It's time for lunch." I was initially unaware of the significance of this behavior and kept encouraging him to pick out another pair of jeans or whatever. His anxiety increased rapidly, and I remember feeling an overwhelming sense of sadness when I realized that "lunch" had to be at noon, not twelve fifteen or twelve thirty. Finally, he became so agitated that we had to leave the store and have lunch immediately, before "it was too late." Clearly, my son was so accustomed to the institution's routine that even a minor deviation caused him extreme anxiety. At that point, I knew I had to get him home soon or I would lose him forever.

Before I could make all the necessary arrangements to get him home, another crisis occurred. Michael was fourteen and growing rapidly. He was much taller than most of the other boys in his unit. One day I received a call from the facility administrator, who informed me that Michael had been arrested for sexually assaulting another resident. I was stunned, because Michael was still very naïve in this area and had not demonstrated any behavior of this type before. I immediately drove to the facility to investigate further. When I arrived, I was not allowed to view the reports, and the staff was uncharacteristically quiet on the matter. I removed Michael and brought him home. Over the next few days, he finally opened up and told me what had happened. His description of the events was quite different from the facility administrator's, and I felt it necessary to hire an attorney in Ohio to investigate the matter further. After several weeks, the truth was finally determined. Michael had been sexually assaulted by a resident, not the other way around. It seems that the other boy, though much smaller than Mike, had in fact been the aggressor. This youngster had been sexually assaulted in his past and was simply engaging in similar actions.

Such behavior is not uncommon for children who suffer sexual abuse. I was very angry with the staff of the facility because they rushed to judgment after talking with both boys and assumed that Michael was the aggressor simply because he was taller and appeared stronger than the other boy. The apologies offered were not sufficient to erase the sense of shame that Michael felt. The entire incident only served to further impact his already low opinion of himself.

I knew I had to get Mike permanently home again as soon as possible. I began the process of working with our local high school toward that end. I also started bringing Mike home for visits rather than continuing to travel to Ohio. I felt it was important to allow him the opportunity to resume his place in our family. The process took much longer than I anticipated, mostly because of the resistance I met at every turn with virtually all school personnel. It was clear that the local school officials were wary about accepting Michael at all. I pushed and pushed because I knew how important it was to my son to attend the local high school just like every other kid in the neighborhood. It was his last chance to prove to himself that he was normal, and after all he had been through, I was determined to give him that chance.

Michael with Sonny on the front lawn

6
Spinning Out of Control

We adore chaos because we love to produce order.

—Unknown

It took almost eight months, but I finally managed to dot all the i's and cross all the t's and Michael returned home on January 10, 1992. Two days later, we celebrated his fifteenth birthday, and I thought we were all thrilled he was home again. As I look back on that time, I think I was so wrapped up in the process of getting him home that I was oblivious to what was going on around me. That's the only thing I can think of to explain the shock I felt when, on January 17, the rest of our "family" asked Michael and I to leave our home. They spoke of growing problems they were having with me, most of which seemed vague. I was unaware of such problems and had absolutely no idea that any of them were struggling with their relationship with me. To add to my confusion, the three adults in our family had just completed the process of remortgaging our home two days earlier. Their decision made no sense to me, and I was devastated. Years later, I came to believe that their decision was based on Michael's return home. Nothing else made sense to me. I believe that in their hearts, they loved Michael very much, but the fact is he was not their son, not their responsibility. I don't think they could face this realization at the time, so they made other excuses for their behavior. Michael certainly was difficult for all of us to live with, and I think that after enjoying more than two years with him away, they could not face what having him return would mean to their daily lives. It took me years to arrive at this explanation, and during that time, I was hurt and angry. They let me down and that was bad enough, but eventually I was able to see what their actions did to my son, and that has proven to be even harder to forgive.

I did not have time to grieve the loss I was experiencing because I had to make decisions and take action quickly. First, I had to find us a place to live. Michael and I moved in with my mother, who lived in a neighboring town, and we remained there for the better part of five months. This was a very stressful time for all three of us. My mother had to adjust to the impulsive whims of an unstable adolescent; Michael struggled to cope with the loss of "family" as he knew it; and I struggled with both issues while working full time, looking for a house, and transporting Mike to and from school every day.

Finally, I was able to purchase a home in the town we had lived in all of Michael's life. It had taken me almost eight months to work out all the particulars associated with his acceptance into the local high school, so I felt we had little choice. I also hoped that returning to the town in which he was raised would help to ease the pain Michael was experiencing over the sudden loss of his home and most of his family.

This was the beginning of some of the hardest days of all. I was clearly alone in parenting Michael now, and these were to be his most difficult years. I was filled with anger and hurt, and I'm sure that there were times when I directed those feelings at my son. His anger was even more extreme, and all of it was directed at me. He blamed me entirely for the break up of our "family," and created a kind of idealized image of the others. This hurt more than I can say, because I felt that I was the only one who hadn't abandoned him, and yet he blamed me for all the hurt he felt. Abandonment issues are prevalent among adopted youngsters, and Michaels' hospitalizations and placement in the residential facility accentuated these issues for him. Now even those who claimed to love him unconditionally had walked away, and I was the only one left standing. Therefore, it made sense that his negative feelings were directed at me. Who else was there? However, this fact did not ease the pain caused by his words and actions. I was scared and getting tired.

In so many ways, Michael was a study in contrasts. Nowhere was this more evident than during his teen years. The anger, frustration, and testing of limits so common at this stage were even more pronounced in a child like Michael. At times, it seemed like he was automatically against anything that was important to me.

In February 1994, our family threw a large party to celebrate my mother's eightieth birthday. We held it in a local restaurant, and dozens of friends and family arrived to share this milestone with a woman who meant a lot to all of us. While my mother, like many of us, had difficulty understanding Michael and dealing with his behavior, she always showed him how much she loved him and accepted him unconditionally as her first grandchild. It was important to me and to her that Mike attend the party. I insisted that he dress up, and I bought him his first sports coat for the occasion. He looked so very handsome that day. For the first hour or so, Mike did well socializing with the other guests, yet I could tell that his social skills were being stretched to the limit. I tried to keep an eye on him throughout the evening so that I could intervene before he made a scene. I realize now that I was expecting trouble because I did not believe that he could sustain appropriate behavior for very long.

Once again, my son surprised me. I was anticipating problems, but what I got instead was a warm sense of pride as he worked very hard to fit in and join the celebration. At one point, I realized that he was nowhere in sight. I could almost feel the sense of panic rising in me. It was at this point that I heard music coming from the room next to us. My sister-in-law and I started to search for Mike and we stuck out heads into the adjacent room to check out the music. Michael was sitting at the piano in front of a completely empty room. He was lost in the music he was creating as he went along. The music was incredibly beautiful. My eyes filled with tears as we quietly closed the door so he would not see that we were there. This was a young man with talent beyond my dreams, more pain than I could ever imagine, and I loved him more each day.

Throughout this text I have described Michael as a "child of extremes." I briefly delineated both the negative or struggling side of the "extreme" and the beautiful and creative side. He was complex and often angry at the world; at the same time he was bright, creative, and compassionate. I told you how handsome he was and that his sense of humor remained a delight to me right up to the day that he died. In addition to his verbal skills and musical talent, Michael demonstrated amazing skill with computers, despite the minimal training he received. He built computers from scratch and created programs for various business or recreational ends. Though his formal education was minimal, he would research computer information and techniques at the local library or through available online resources. Then he would apply this newfound knowledge to the problem at hand until he was able to find a workable solution. I often wonder how far these innate abilities could have taken him—just one of the many questions to which there will never be an answer.

Perhaps my favorite part of Michael was his compassion for others. Not many people saw that part of him, so I feel lucky to be one who was privy to it often. Even as a small child, he sensed pain in others and offered a smile, a hand, or a kind word in return.

For most of my adult career, I worked with young people incarcerated in a juvenile detention facility. The Christmas holidays were always a particularly difficult time for these kids and their families. My assistant and I routinely tried to ease this pressure during the holidays while at the same time encouraging our own families to see Christmas as a time of giving. Each year our two families spent a part of Christmas Eve at the youth facility. We prepared and served a meal that almost any teenager would love. These kids only ate a rather institutionalized menu, so we tried hard to provide one special meal that was as far from that as possible. Usually our effort included such things as tacos or sloppy joes, ice-cream sundaes, a variety of candy, and all the pop any of them could drink.

One particular year stands out in my mind. It was not uncommon for our facility to house youngsters with a wide variety of physical and mental problems. This particular year we housed a young man with cerebral palsy accused of a rather serious felony. Clearly, he wasn't going to receive a furlough for the holidays. Often this young man ate at a time that was different from the population at large because the staff had to feed him and he had considerable difficulty swallowing. In addition, we tried hard not to make him any more of a spectacle than was necessary in a facility filled with emotionally challenging adolescents. When feeding him, some of the food would make it into his mouth, but some would also run down his chin. The process of feeding him was long and often tedious, both for him and his caretaker. Despite these challenges, we wanted him to enjoy the special treats offered at the Christmas Eve meal.

I remember we were all set up with Crock-Pots full of sloppy joes, and the kids were going through the line filling their plates with all kinds of goodies. At one point, I looked up and there was Michael sitting with the young disabled teen. He and Jason, one of my assistant's sons, were obviously drawn to this young man who was sitting alone at a large table. They had taken it upon themselves to help this youngster with absolutely no guidance from the adults in charge. Michael was spoon-feeding this resident, and Jason would gently wipe his chin as the food dribbled down. They were chatting with him throughout this process. Both Jason's mom and I were deeply touched by this experience. Here were two teenage boys on their own taking on the difficult task of feeding a severely disabled teen instead of interacting with the other "normal" youngsters in our care. They could see that he needed help, and before any of the adults could step in, they rose to the challenge. The kindness and compassion they both showed that day was a clear indication to all of us of the quality of their character. Both these young men experienced significant hardship growing up. Perhaps the depth of their individual struggle was exactly the reason they were drawn to help a disabled youngster enjoy such a rare event.

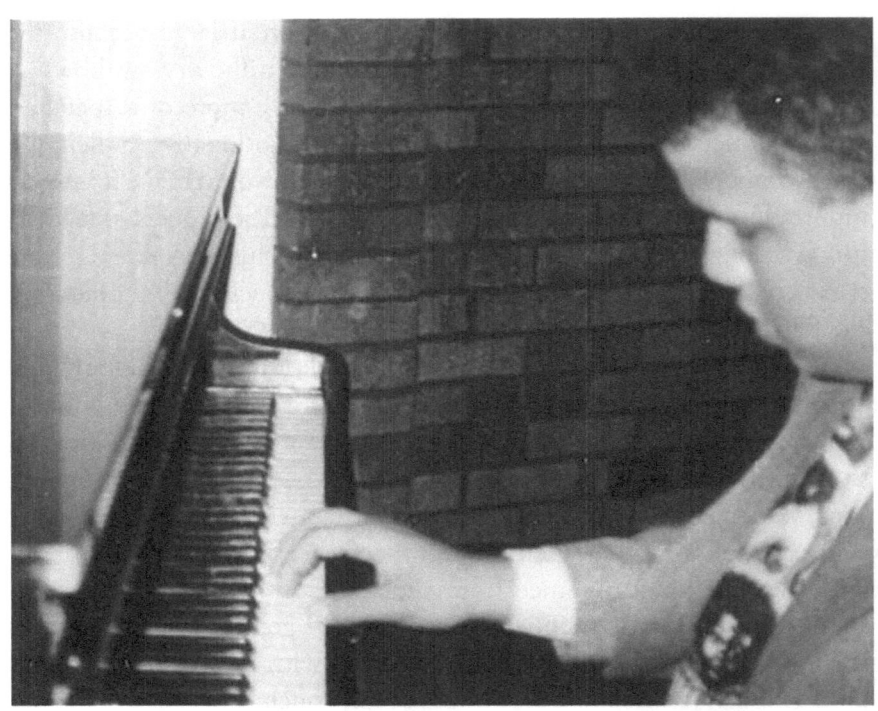

Michael composing music, age seventeen.

I have many precious memories of Michael reaching out to others. Often the compassion and understanding he demonstrated went way beyond his years. I treasure those memories because they, more than anything else, exposed who he really was inside, the child I loved more than life itself.

Although it was a daily struggle for both of us, later that year Michael graduated from high school as planned. He was seventeen years old, and like many adolescents, had absolutely no idea where he wanted life to take him. He went from one dead-end job to another, spending increasing amounts of time in the basement of our home, sometimes with friends, often alone. He had absolutely no clear sense of direction. Continuing in school was not something he wanted to pursue. His only passion seemed to center around computers, particularly video games. He spent countless hours on the computer, especially very late at night and into the early morning hours. Then he would sleep most of the day away, and the pattern would continue all over again.

I tried to set limits regarding employment, chores around the house, and general behavior and attitude. Michael continued to test these limits at every turn, and after nearly a year of continued daily stress, I finally reached the end of my patience. I told him he had to leave. I knew he had nowhere to go, but I could no longer tolerate his emotional and verbal abuse. Knowing he had no alternative and that I was not capable of physically forcing him to do anything, he refused to leave. I realized that this was just another attempt on his part to test my limits, and I knew I had no good alternative but to follow through on my threat. It was at that point that I called the police for assistance.

While on the phone, the officer asked me if Michael had a weapon, and I assured her that no weapons were involved. Michael was listening to my side of the conversation, and at that point, he picked up a steak knife from the kitchen sink. The officer heard me tell him to put it down. When the police entered our home, Michael fled out the back door, and because of the exchange the officer had heard on the phone, the police chased him with their weapons drawn. I watched out my living room window in horror as they threw my son to the ground, handcuffed him, and took him into custody. My heart broke that day, but I didn't know what else to do. I felt like I was going down with him, and as the only responsible adult in the daily picture, I had to step away and regain some control over myself or I could never help him to heal. I could feel my strength waning. I was so very tired.

He returned later that day with the police. He packed a few things and left without a word. I tried to find out his plans, but he was not about to ease my mind, and the fact is, I don't think he had any. He walked off that day, and I didn't hear from him for a couple of weeks. This was the first of several times when anger and frustration separated us. He called on his eighteenth birthday to ask if I would pick him up at the train station. I did. I remember that when he got in my car, he talked about the fact that he had informed his fellow passengers on the train that it was his birthday, and they all sang and congratulated him. He seemed genuinely pleased with himself. All I could think was how incredibly sad it was that he thought so little of himself. He came home that day, and the struggle to find a way to live together continued.

For a short time, life was calm, and I was just glad to have him home. However, as soon as I started placing expectations on him, the struggle resumed. Having survived on his own for a brief time, he was now convinced that he really didn't need me at all, so once I pushed him to demonstrate more responsibility, he took off again. It was late January 1995. We had had an argument the night before because I insisted that he get a job and stop just lying around the house playing video games. I went to bed that night expecting the struggle to continue the next morning, but when I got up, he was gone. There was no note, no indication of where he was going. He simply packed up his things and left. I felt sure that, like the last time, he wouldn't be gone long, and I would once again get a call asking for help.

A few weeks later, I turned fifty, and friends and family planned a surprise party for me. I had overheard enough to have some vague idea of the plan, but I had no idea how I was going to get through it. I could not even imagine acting happy. The truth was I was terrified. Though he always talked like he had significant life experience, Michael was even more naïve than his age indicated. I was so afraid that he would trust the wrong people and somehow get himself into serious trouble, either physically, legally, or both. All I could do was pray that he was alive and would contact me soon.

I came home from work one day, and he was sitting on the couch. We talked a bit, and once again he made the promises I wanted to hear. For a time, life was calm, and once again, I was just glad to have him home. He looked for work and succeeded in finding low-paying jobs without any future. This was fine with me, because he was at least showing some effort and he was home. As the weeks went on, his agitation grew as he searched for his place in this world. In the summer of 1995, Michael suddenly announced he was joining the army. I was hesitant to support such a direction at first, but I quickly fell into the trap of believing that maybe this was an answer. I convinced myself that the structure and discipline the military required might really help Mike to get his life in order. I let myself think that maybe this was the answer to my prayers. It was not.

Michael was scheduled to report on October 1, 1995, but the day before my mother died of cancer. She was the only grandparent he had ever known, and I felt it was important for him to remain with his family through the service. I contacted the recruiting officer and informed him of the circumstances. Michael was allowed to report on

October 4, the day after attending his grandmother's funeral. I knew the loss of his grandmother would be difficult for Michael, but he assured me that he was fine and left for the army as scheduled. In a matter of just a few hours, I said good-bye to my mother and my son. It was not an easy time, but I so wanted Michael to succeed that I hid my sadness until after he left.

Before a month had passed, I received a call from his commanding officer to inform me that they were sending Michael home. It was clear to them that he was not emotionally stable enough to continue. We both agreed that perhaps he was too young, and the officer encouraged me to have him wait a couple of years before even attempting to re-enter the service.

Michael returned home angrier than he left. Verbally he always blamed someone or something else for any problem that he faced, but I knew him well enough to know that in his heart, he blamed himself for every failure he encountered, both real and imaginary. Over the next few months, his behavior was erratic. At times, he was sad and depressed, and other times he was impulsive and angry. The only constant was that he never seemed happy.

Once again, we returned to the usual cycle of no work or working at low-paying jobs that went nowhere. This cycle was always accompanied by some quiet times mixed with angry outbursts. Michael had been in therapy before, and I insisted that he return if he wanted to live in our home. The therapist worked diligently with him toward improved self-esteem and tried to help him work through his pervasive feelings of abandonment. In my head, I knew that part of Michael was trying to push me away so that I too would leave him as every other significant adult in his life had done. Many a day I wished that I had that option. However, the truth was that I needed him as much as he needed me. He was my son, we were a family, and at some level, we were all each other had in this world.

I wanted my son to be happy more than anything, and I continued to pray for the wisdom to guide him in a direction that would bring him success. He was so very talented, and yet he was his own worst enemy. Every time it seemed that he was making progress in the world, he would find a way to sabotage his own efforts. And so the cycle continued.

7
The Cycle Continues

Normal is nothing more than a cycle on a washing machine.

—Whoopi Goldberg

After a number of months working in minimum wage jobs, Michael expressed an interest in continuing his education, and we found a residential junior college that would accept him despite his poor academic record. Although Michael was very bright, his lack of self-discipline never allowed him to succeed academically. I remember being so pleased to find a school in central Illinois that seemed to be perfect for a kid like Mike; that is, a young person who definitely had the intellectual ability to succeed in school but lacked the maturity and emotional stability to responsibly handle the academic world.

Looking back on this period, I can see how much I was again kidding myself that perhaps this was an answer. I knew how bright he was and had hopes that he would actually become excited about learning at the college level. I allowed myself to fall into the excitement that any parent feels when helping to get her child ready for college. I bought him clothes, bedding, and all the usual supplies. I so wanted him to succeed, to be normal, that I made myself believe he was ready when all the signs clearly indicated otherwise. I did not want to see them; they contradicted the reality that I so desperately wanted to believe in. So I pushed forward despite the warnings that flooded my mind, and he left for school in the fall.

He was only there a few weeks when I received a late night call from the dean telling me that I had to come to the school and take him home. He said Mike was not getting along with the other students and was a constant disruption in the dorm. He informed me that Michael had been involved in some kind of fight that evening. I remember him describing the scene as there being "blood everywhere." He sounded desperate and frantic, and it was clear to me that I had no choice. Even though I was not aware of the specifics at the time, I was not worried about Michael having caused injury to others. Despite his size and strength, Michael never was violent with anyone but himself. As I received more information from the dean, it became clear that the blood he spoke of resulted from Michael deliberately hurting himself. No one else was injured. I left as soon as possible and once again brought him home.

As in the past, Michael's verbal comments over the next several weeks centered on blaming others for what occurred. It was clear that internally, he blamed himself for what must have seemed to him to be yet another failure. His depression was a constant concern, so he returned to therapy with a professional who had considerable experience with youth. In retrospect, I'm sure this treatment helped, but he still struggled a great deal. The weeks that followed were full of more anger and conflict. The counselor helped me understand that what Michael demonstrated as anger was often actually fear, an emotion he simply did not allow himself to acknowledge. I tried to keep that in mind so as not to overreact to the angry words and actions directed at me. Sometimes I succeeded, but often I did not.

The up and down cycle of our life continued throughout this time period. There were calm times, which I relished, and then there were angry fights over the same old issues. Several times, Michael enrolled in various courses at our local junior college. He experienced considerable success in all computer-related courses and in any subject that required him to express himself in writing. However, he was never able to complete the other required courses for an associate's degree.

These moments of success occurred during periods of ongoing failure. His anger continued to be a serious problem for him and for me, which resulted in him leaving home two more times during this period. These episodes were more serious than his other ventures, and my fear for his safety increased.

After he returned that second time, it was only a short time before the pattern began again. This time he could feel my patience waning and left home on his own before I reached the point of pushing him out the door. This time was also different because he was gone for months without a word.

I was sure I would hear from him at Christmas, partly because he had already been gone for several weeks, but mostly because he so loved the holidays. Some of my most precious memories center on those Christmas mornings when it was just the two of us. He was always so excited, although he tried hard not to show it through his teen years. I just knew he would make it home for Christmas, or at least he would call and let me know he was okay. That Christmas came and went, and I never heard from him. The sadness I felt was surpassed only by my fear. I realized that I had no way of knowing if he was even alive. My mind played cruel tricks on me. I convinced myself that he had identification on him. If something happened to him, someone would find me, wouldn't they? I had no idea where he was, how he was surviving, or why he felt it necessary separate from me so completely. Looking back on those months, the not knowing was the most painful part of all.

I kept working each day and tried to continue with my life, such as it was. But by the time Michael was gone for almost four months and I still had no idea where he was, I was terrified that something terrible had happened to him.

Finally, I received a call from a hospital in Minnesota. Michael was there with an injured ankle, and they had encouraged him to call home. The injury was minor, and I was elated that he was okay. I arranged to get him home.

For a couple of weeks he just hung around the house, giving his ankle ample time to heal. I later learned that Michael had become involved with a company that apparently preyed on young, often homeless, adolescents, sending them out to sell magazines all over the country.

They provided minimum wages and paid a small stipend toward food and housing. Virtually all of the individual's wages must go to pay for the remainder of the hotel bills and fast food costs, which left them with nothing. These young people were trapped into remaining with the company because the lack of money left them no way out. Michael had sprained his ankle while selling magazines in a neighborhood in southern Minnesota. The company would not pay for any medical attention, so he was on his own. The hospital, of course, wanted some guarantee of payment, so they called me. It was the best phone call I had received in years, and I gladly encouraged them to send me the bill. I often wonder about all the young people out there trapped in similar or worse circumstances; youngsters whose parents have no idea where they are and perhaps don't even care. What a cruel way to learn that life is not always like the fairy tales we read as children. So many of these young people, like my son, physically look like adults but are more like children than we realize.

In little time, Michael returned to his usual pattern. He worked for a while, things were good for a while, and then the anger and frustration once again took center stage. We both were growing so very tired of this pattern, but it seemed impossible to break.

Finally, the constant turmoil, angry outbursts, and verbal abuse were more than I could tolerate, and I told him once again to leave our home. He had virtually nothing but an old broken-down car that I knew would not last. But I also knew that continuing to allow him to drift through life and drain me of money, energy, and hope was not teaching him the life lessons he so desperately needed to learn. So I watched him pack what little he owned and walk out into the world again with absolutely no place to go. He had burned so many bridges behind him that any resources beyond his family were also gone. I had no idea where he would go or what he would do, and I'm sure he didn't either.

Once again, months passed without word. Apparently, he just wandered from state to state, picking up odd jobs, sleeping in his car and generally drifting to nowhere. Eventually he made his way back to our town and joined the ranks of the homeless. One day at work, someone mentioned to me that he had seen a homeless person that looked a lot like Michael wandering the streets of our downtown area.

I don't recall what, if anything, I said, but I do remember my reaction to such an announcement. Once again, my feelings were ambivalent, ranging from excitement and anticipation to general fear and dread, from hope and relief to embarrassment and despair. As soon as my colleague mentioned this sighting, I knew it was Michael. There was no doubt in my mind. I later found out that it was in fact him, and he was wandering the county, going from shelter to shelter, as is the lot of all the homeless in our community.

I knew the director of the homeless program in our area, and I was quite sure that she would know Michael if he appeared on her doorstep. In addition, knowing the services her program provided, I was confident that his most basic needs were being met. However, despite this knowledge, I couldn't help myself. I left work each day during the lunch break and drove through our downtown area, near the shelter, hoping to see my son. One day I spotted him walking through town, and I was shocked by his appearance. Despite the warm summer temperature, he was clothed in several layers, covered by his army jacket, which I recognized immediately. His hair was long and looked both dirty and uncombed. I had never seen him with a beard before and the overall picture brought me to tears. I kept driving while watching him in my rearview mirror. No mother should ever have to see such a sight. I was overwhelmed.

The next few weeks just dragged on for me. I was so torn. Nevertheless, somewhere inside of me I knew that I had to allow this struggle to continue at his pace. I had to wait for him to be ready to come home and respect me as well as the rules of the house. Therefore, I waited. Finally, early one Saturday morning, my doorbell rang. When I opened the door, I was greeted by a tall, elderly police officer who stood next to my son. Michael could not even look at me, but rather stood there with his head down staring at the ground.

The police officer asked if they could come in. We sat at my dining room table, and the officer proceeded to tell me that he had met Michael several weeks earlier. He found him sleeping in a cardboard box behind one of the stores in our local shopping area. Apparently, they had several talks, and the officer was convinced that Michael had learned many of life's hardest lessons. The officer begged me to let Michael come home. Up to this point, Mike had been silent, still unable to look at me. This was one of many times that my faith took over. I didn't have the strength to speak the words that followed on my own. I just wanted my son home again and was too tired to continue the fight. God was with me that morning when I heard myself confidently tell the officer that while I loved my son and would welcome him home with open arms, I had no choice but to insist on a significant change in behavior before such a reunion could occur. He said he understood and turned to Michael.

The officer reminded Mike that he needed to convince me that he was ready to return home. After a couple of minutes of silence, Michael finally began to speak. His voice choked and his eyes teared up as he asked me to please let him come home. He promised to respect me and my property, and vowed that he would get a job as soon as possible. He paused a couple of times. I forced myself to remain silent, though it was hard not to just give in. I knew that he had to say more in order to feel my determination to make this work once and for all.

He talked about knowing now that what I required of him was more than fair, and that he was the one who needed to change. He said he understood what was expected and would follow the rules and help around the house. He knew me well enough to know that the most important thing I required was that he show me the respect every parent deserves, and he promised that he would. My heart was so full that morning. It was almost easy to forget all the pain and just allow the joy and relief to prevail. Michael was safe, and he was home.

Much later, I would discover that during that period of being homeless, Michael met a young man named Chris and through Chris connected with a group of young men who would eventually become his lifelong friends. Throughout his life, making and keeping friends was always difficult for Mike. His erratic and impulsive behavior, coupled with his intensity, often scared others and sent kids fleeing from his attempts at friendship. He was in his early twenties at that point and had rarely experienced the kind of friendship that could withstand the stresses of life. I speak more about these friends later, but I wanted to mention that Michael received this gift at the lowest point in his young life.

By this time, I had a much better understanding of Michael's disabilities. I knew that his brain simply didn't work like everyone else's. Even while he was talking, I knew that these promises would not last. Yet I kept remembering something that one of his doctors told me many years earlier. He said, "Even though you know he cannot always meet them, you must set the standards for appropriate behavior, because if you don't, he will never understand what normal is." That made a lot of sense to me at the time, and even though it was hard to do, I knew that loving Michael meant that I had to teach him step by step what appropriate behavior was. In addition, I had to repeat the lessons over and over for him to internalize them. The conversation at my dining room table early that Saturday morning was just another step in that process. So I welcomed my son home that morning, and we moved on with our life together, not knowing then that we had very little time left.

The next couple of years are just a blur for me. I want so badly to remember every minute I spent with my son, but the truth is that I can't. Living with Michael was like being on a perpetual roller coaster, and sometimes I just closed my eyes and waited for the next dip. I do remember that he made additional efforts at school. He took several more classes at the local junior college. I kept telling myself that maybe this time something would work, and he would wake up one day, realize how incredibly bright he was, and his life would just take off. It never happened. He played around at college, taking a course or two here and there. Sometimes he did remarkably well, other times he dropped classes and just coasted. He kept going from hopeless job to hopeless job. I often kidded that at one time or another he had worked at every retail store at the local mall. But the truth was, it wasn't very funny. Michael was in his early twenties and just floating through life, with absolutely no idea where he wanted to be and even less insight as to how to get there.

I felt truly helpless during these years. I couldn't seem to help him. He continued to go to therapy, but it seemed to me that the most it did was help him keep his overwhelming anger in check. Michael always seemed so very angry. He argued with everyone about anything. He woke up angry and went to bed the same way. He rarely smiled during these years. I was so tired of fighting, pushing, cajoling, bribing, and praying that I sort of coasted through these years too. My energy was waning. I was so tired, and I often felt like I was running out of time.

Michael spent a lot of time with his friends during this period, though I really didn't get to know these young people very well until years later. He had more girlfriends than I could count and seemed to move between them with ease. However, there was only one young girl who seemed to matter to him. I think she was his first (and perhaps only) true love. I remember how happy he was when their relationship first started to flourish. They talked on the phone for hours. He paced around the house, waiting for the clock to reach the time he was to leave to pick her up. For a short time, he seemed happy, and I relish those memories.

I remember one cold February evening. It was my birthday. Michael rarely remembered my birthday, so I didn't expect anything from him. He must have mentioned it to his girlfriend, and she was determined they would find an inexpensive way to surprise me. I left work and walked to my car. When I opened the door, I found my car so filled with balloons, I could hardly get in it. There was a card taped to the steering wheel. It was from Mike, and I was stunned. He had never done anything like that before. I'm sure it was his girlfriend's influence, but I cherish the memory anyway. He didn't have to follow her suggestion, but he did, and I loved it.

Unfortunately for all concerned, that relationship did not last, although they always remained good friends. Mike went from girl to girl after that, and each one seemed more disturbed than the last. Sometimes I thought he was attracted to girls who he saw as more dysfunctional than he was. Michael was very familiar with his weaknesses and deficiencies. I only wish he had also been as knowledgeable about his strengths. He was such a handsome young man, his humor was delightful, his laughter infectious. Throughout his life, I was amazed by his mind and how quickly he learned, retained, and applied information. Unfortunately, he never was able to use those abilities to win the conflict that raged within him.

Eventually I could see that he was losing the battle. He became more and more depressed. He spent far too many hours in the darkened spaces of our basement, often alone. When he was not working, he slept during the day and spent nights alone, watching TV, using the computer or playing video games. Eventually this self-loathing began to take the form of cutting. On several occasions, he cut himself repeatedly up and down his arms. I would find bloody towels in the washing machine and could see the scabs and scars on his arms. I tried speaking to him about this behavior, but always to no avail. I was overwhelmed. I had finally reached the point where I had absolutely no idea how to help my son. I just wanted to hide. I could feel his depression all around. It permeated our home. I felt like I too was suffocating.

Occasionally there was some light during these hard years. He would seem to make progress, maybe get new job, sometimes a new girlfriend, or often just a productive conversation between us. There would be a ray of hope, and we both would cling to it. Then the darkness would return, with more crises, more sadness, and then despair.

8
A Child's Gift

The greatest gift is a portion of thyself.
                              —Ralph Waldo Emerson

Near the end of this terribly hard period, I was set to retire. The time
was right, the offer was too attractive to pass up, and I was ready for
a rest. The plan was to retire on June 21, 2001 after twenty-nine years
working with delinquent youth and their families. I had mixed feelings
about this stage of my life. I was certainly ready to retire, but I was
afraid of what life would be like if Michael was still at home and we
were together even more than we had been before. His depression was so
contagious, and I feared that I would get caught up in it and no longer
be able to help either of us.

My coworkers planned a retirement party in my honor, and I was
thoroughly excited about the upcoming event. I gave them the names of
various professional colleagues who I wanted them to invite as speakers.
I also provided a list of friends and family members I wanted included.
These were all people who had significantly impacted my career in
one way or another. Just a few days before the party, I discovered that
Michael had also been asked to speak. I was shocked. I knew full well
what his mood had been like, and I had no idea if he could find the

strength to speak in front of so many people about anything, let alone about his mother. I begged my assistant to change the program. I really didn't think my son could handle such an emotionally stressful situation. For the rest of my life I will regret that I did not believe enough in the strength of my own son. He did speak that day, and he was amazing. He stood up on the stage, and his voice was strong and proud. He spoke of what my dedication to my work had taught him. He was articulate and genuine, and I loved him for having the courage to speak out. I cried many tears that day, tears of joy and pride, not for me, but for a young man who never ceased to amaze me. Once again he was my "child of extremes," not so much a child anymore, but always able to rise to the occasion. A colleague of mine had the presence of mind to video tape this event for me, now I have a tape of my son telling the world that he was proud of his mother—what better gift!

Michael was twenty-four years old when I retired. He was still living at home and moving from job to job with little sense of direction. As I mentioned earlier, I was concerned about how we would manage in the house together when I was no longer working. We did have some ups and downs in those last couple of years. But something was different, less intense, perhaps less angry.

I know when someone we love dies, we tend to remember more of the good than the bad, and I guess that's a good thing. I find this is especially true about the last years of his life. Those final two years, for example, there were still problems, arguments, and angry shouting matches. However, I remember more of the good about those days, and I am grateful for that gift.

I felt that in order for Michael to make any determined progress in his life, he needed to live on his own, away from me. Therefore, in the fall of 2002, I set a time limit for him, indicating that he had to be out of the house by the first of the year. I told him I would help with initial payments for rent and so forth, but he had to find a place, sign a lease, and begin to live by the rules of the world around him, not just those of our home.

In November 2002, I took a wonderful vacation to Italy. It was the trip of a lifetime. I went with several of my Italian cousins to return to the birthplace of our ancestors. When I returned home, Michael announced that he wanted to move to Colorado, a state more than a thousand miles from our home. At first I was stunned, as this had never come up as an option before. I knew he had a friend that had moved out there, but he never mentioned he wanted to go. In addition, I was worried that Colorado was just too far. I figured that Michael would still have ups and downs, and it would be much more difficult to help him from such a distance. Then it dawned on me! Perhaps that was the whole point. Michael always demonstrated far more insight than one would ascribe to him given his comments and behavior. Perhaps he understood that in order to be independent, he had to be far away from me. Far enough away that he could not easily knock on my door and ask for money to help him out of his latest jam. He knew himself well enough to see that in order to rely on himself, he had to have some distance. I am not sure if this is true, but it feels good to believe, so what's the harm?

It was December, and I funded a trip for him to Colorado to check out jobs and housing. In retrospect, I must have been out of my mind. Traveling to Colorado at that time of year with an old, unreliable car; what was I thinking to support such a journey? Nevertheless, he went, and the trip was a remarkable success. He did not find a job, but there were a number of possibilities. He did find an affordable apartment, and he signed a one-year lease.

He returned home and began the process of packing up his life to head west. The plan was to hitch a trailer and begin the long drive across the country right after Christmas. He had a friend who was going to help him with the drive, and he had a place to stay until the apartment was available on the first of the year.

With very little effort, I can still actually see him in my mind's eye. He is standing in our garage, finishing the packing of the trailer. He is standing there in his black leather jacket with his Chicago Cubs hat. It's around eleven o'clock at night on December 26. He is walking toward me to say good-bye. I can still almost feel his hug, and he looks at me and says, "Thanks for everything, Mom." I hug him back, kiss him good-bye, and he's gone.

Michael had come and gone several times before that night, but this time was different. He was not leaving in anger. I was not throwing him out the door. There was something different about his words as well. I knew at the time that he didn't just mean thanks for the money I had slipped him for the trip or thanks for paying for the hitch and trailer. He didn't just mean thanks for helping with the security deposit and first month's rent. He meant "Thanks for everything," and somehow I understood that even then. His words touched my heart that cold night, as we stood in our garage and said good-bye. Of course, I thought I was simply saying "Good-bye son, have a great life, be happy, make me proud." Little did I know that this truly was good-bye.

Michael in Louisiana with friends

He drove straight through and arrived safely in Colorado. He was able to get into his new apartment a few days early, and he began his life away from home. He got a job quickly, and his girlfriend moved in with him. She was a girl from Arizona whom he had met on the Internet. I knew nothing about her, but this was his life, not mine. He called frequently to fill me in on what was going on, and I loved his calls. For the most part, he actually sounded happy. I could almost see him smiling as he recounted the latest events in his life. I was thrilled.

Late one Friday afternoon in March, I was playing bridge with some friends at my dining room table when the doorbell rang. I was stunned when I opened the door and there stood my son with his new girlfriend. I had not expected him and had no idea why he was here. He introduced me to his girl, and said he needed to pick up a few things and was only staying for a very brief visit because he was due back at work at 11:00 pm on Sunday. I remember returning to the card table, making comments to my friends about how foolish he was to drive fourteen hours home when he had to be back at work the day after tomorrow. We all laughed at the impulsive decisions often made by young people, and got on with our card game. I realized much later that Mike was home to show off his girlfriend and the brand new car he had purchased in Colorado. It was as if his life was starting to resemble something normal, and he could not wait to have me see the progress he was making. Of course, I had no way of knowing at the time that that was the last time I would ever see my son.

They stayed overnight and spent time with his friends. On Saturday evening, they were ready to hit the road again when Michael stopped and asked me if I thought his aunt and uncle might be home. Since it was a Saturday evening, I had no idea and told him so. He called and they were home. He told them he wanted to drop by to say hello, and they encouraged him to do so. I knew he wanted to show off a bit, and I figured with the progress he was making, he had earned it. So off they went. That brief visit was the last my brother would ever see of Michael, and I know he remembers it fondly.

9
The Beginning of the End

Just as the body goes into shock after a physical trauma,
so does the human psyche go into shock
after the impact of a major loss.

—Anne Grant

I spent most of my career working in the criminal justice system and frequently saw the horrors that can result from the combination of children and guns. I never allowed guns in my home, not even the kind you play with. I felt that guns should never be viewed as toys. I made a clear exception with squirt guns, but that was as far as I would go. I often wonder now if I made too much of it, thereby making guns even more attractive to my son. I never purchased toy guns for him and did not allow others to do so either. At times he pleaded with me, but I held my ground. Sometimes he would even try to fashion a gun out of scrap wood he found in the garage.

It turns out that purchasing a firearm was probably one of the first things Michael did after he moved out on his own. I didn't know this at the time, and of course, it was not something he offered to tell me. In addition, apparently owning a gun and showing it off to others increased his self-esteem in some distorted way. Although he was twenty-five years old when he left home, in some ways, he was twenty-five going on fifteen. He still had occasions when he acted without thinking through the possible consequences. Eventually, such immature, impulsive behavior cost him his life.

I was sound asleep at three fifteen in the morning on May 8, 2003, when the shrill ring of my telephone jolted me out of bed. Calls in the middle of the night are never good, and I braced myself for bad news about my brother. For some strange reason I never even thought about Michael. It was not an out of sight, out of mind kind of thing, because our children are never really out of mind no matter where they live. Rather, it was a belief that he was doing so well. We had talked the previous afternoon, and he sounded so happy. He had good job prospects, seemed so pleased to have his own place, and I was so very happy for him.

I picked up the phone and heard the voice of Gabe, one of Michael's friends. He informed me that I had to call Mike's girlfriend on Michael's cell phone immediately. It was such an odd request. Why wouldn't I call Michael on his phone? Why was I calling anyone at this hour? Gabe didn't know. He simply said that he had received a call from Colorado. Michael's girlfriend, Stephanie, was hysterical and asked him to get me to call immediately.

I got up and went downstairs. I paced the floor repeatedly. I was both afraid to make the call and anxious to find out what was happening at the same time. Finally, I called and Stephanie answered. Once she realized that it was me, she just kept screaming, "Are you ready for this?" over and over again. I remember asking her to calm down and tell me what was wrong. There was a pause, and then she said the words that every parent dreads: "Michael is dead." She went on to explain some of the details, but I was only half listening. I felt dizzy and nauseous. The walls of my home were closing in; I found it hard to breathe. This could not really be happening. As I refocused on Stephanie's words, I heard her say that I was going to receive a call from the Arapahoe County Sheriff's Department. I couldn't listen anymore, and I just abruptly hung up. I had to catch my breath. I felt like I was suffocating. I was alone in the house, it was three thirty in the morning, and my only child was dead. How could that be? I had just spoken to him twelve hours ago. He sounded happy, excited even. He had a job interview the next morning, and he was sure he would get the job. I can still hear the end of our conversation. When I was ready to hang up, as always I said, "I love you, honey." He came back with his usual response, "Love you too, Mom." Those were the last words he ever said to me.

Eventually the phone rang, and it was a social worker from the Arapahoe County Sheriff's Department. I remember her saying how sorry she was to have to tell me this over the phone. She went on to tell me that Michael was dead at the scene of his apartment. Apparently, there was a party with lots of alcohol, and, according to others present, Michael was showing off his new gun. The bullets were on the counter, so clearly he thought it was unloaded. However, there were only five bullets, because one had already entered the chamber. Everyone present, including Michael, seemed to be too intoxicated to notice. Michael continued to joke around and he pulled the trigger, shooting himself in the head. He died instantly.

As I listened to the tragic details, I could imagine it happening just as I was hearing it. It sounded like something that an immature, impulsive Michael would do. I had so hoped that he was beyond such behavior. Now I knew he was not and he never would be. Now I knew that his impulsive behavior had finally cost him his life.

I was so overwhelmed that I could not think straight. Finally, I asked the social worker what I was to do. She immediately responded that I could have his body cremated and returned home for a burial service. I remember screaming that no one was to touch his body. I had to see my son; I had to make sure it was him. She told me how to arrange to have his body flown home, and I hung up.

Throughout my education, I had studied grief and its various stages. According to experts like Elisabeth Kubler-Ross, I knew that denial was the first step in a long and painful process. Yet in those first moments, I must admit, my initial reaction was a bizarre kind of acceptance. For those first few minutes, sitting alone in my dining room, I knew it was true. He was gone, and I would never see that smile again. The denial came soon after, but for those first few minutes, I knew my son was dead.

I called my brother and sister-in-law, and it seemed like only moments later they were knocking on my door. They came to grieve with me, hold me, take care of me, and I will love them for it until the day that I die. I realized many months later that, even though you are initially numb at such a tragic point in your life, it is impossible to forget the words and actions of those around you. It is as if their voices and behaviors are permanently etched in your brain. I think part of the reason for this is that as the months go by, you need to replay such memories over and over again just to survive.

In retrospect, I am not at all sure I would have survived the tragic loss of my only child, my only immediate family, had it not been for the loving response of my brother and sister-in-law early that morning and the many friends who sustained me in the months and years to come.

I simply cannot forget the people who were there for me and likewise, I have not yet been able to forgive those who were not. On an intellectual level, I understand why some people respond poorly in times of such tragedy. I know it's hard to find the "right words." The loss of a child is so devastating that it simply makes us all cling to our own children in a vain attempt to protect them and ourselves from such a tragedy. In addition, the suddenness of this loss frightens us all and graphically reminds us that life is indeed fragile. No matter how young or healthy we may be, the next breath could be our last. No one wants to focus on such frightening realities. Therefore, it is easier to ignore, just send a card, write a check, attend the wake, and leave as soon as possible. We all know there are no "right words" to say anyway, so some just go through the motions to make the fear tragedy brings go away.

I understand these reactions, but understanding is not enough. I remember almost every word spoken to me in those early days. I remember who called, who came over, who offered to help, and who helped without offering. These truths are etched in my mind forever.

He died at 11:24 pm on May 7, 2003. I buried him on Tuesday, May 13, at the end of the longest week in my life. It took three full days to get his body home. Part of that was the distance and part was the need for a police investigation due to the nature of his death. He arrived at O'Hare airport around 10:00 pm on Saturday, May 10. I had already determined that the wake would be delayed until Monday because Sunday was Mother's Day and I refused to wake my son on Mother's Day. As it turned out, Mother's Day was the first opportunity I had to view his body. How do you process the sight of your own child lying lifeless in front of you? I remember reaching out and touching his arm in an effort to make the sight more real. He was really there, it was really him. Physically he was a grown man, filling every corner of that coffin, but at first, all I saw was a skinny little kid. I wanted to reach in, lift him up, and carry him home. Thankfully, those moments are fleeting, and the true reality sets in very quickly.

The funeral home was full throughout the evening, and I remember thinking how grateful I was that so many people loved me and my family. So many people made the effort to attend this service and respectfully support me in my effort to survive this tragedy. I was and still am grateful for their kindness.

Some individuals stand out in my mind. There was my cousin, who came early and remained throughout the evening until the wake was over. He sat at the very back of the funeral home, and every time my eye caught his, he smiled and gave a little wave. The message was "I'm still here just in case you need anything. I am not going anywhere. I'm here for you, and I'll stay until you leave." His strength kept me standing that day, and I will love him forever for the gift of his presence.

One friend brought food for the wake, took care of so many details, and watched over me with loving care. There was another friend who even brought an overnight bag and moved in with me, simply announcing, "This is not a time for you to be alone." She did my laundry, made coffee, answered the door, served lunch, and cleaned the kitchen. She was there to cry with me late at night and to sit silently when no words could ease the pain. How could I ever forget such cherished friends?

There was Michael's friend, Ryan, who stood at the front of the funeral home and sobbed as the reality of death impacted him with a force he never expected. He just could not believe that his young friend would be gone forever.

There were friends of mine who had lost children of their own. They came and held me, and I knew they understood as no one else could. They watched over me with delicate, loving care and I survived.

There was the friend from out of town who surprised me by showing up the morning of the funeral after driving for ten hours to be with me and my family and help us cope with this tragedy. His gift will long be remembered.

There was the friend who spoke at the funeral. He loved Michael almost as much as he loved his own two sons. He had helped raise my son, offered him guidance, fun activities, and stern direction when needed. I will never forget how much he gave to me and to my son throughout the good years and the bad.

There was Michael's good friend, Neil, who asked my permission to place something in the casket as a symbol of the connection he and others felt to my son. Bryan, another close friend of Michael's, spoke at the funeral. He rose with courage and determination, and spoke of his friendship with my son. His comments were at times humorous, and his effort even brought a smile to my face when I didn't think I would ever smile again.

The funeral was the next day, and several of Michael's friends were pallbearers. Those young men dressed in white shirts and ties, some in suits or sports coats, all looked so very young. I will never forget the sight of them bringing my son to the altar. They acted with such respect and dignity. I hope and pray that someday they will all understand what a gift they gave me that day. Their presence allowed me to say good-bye to Michael and walk away that warm and sunny May afternoon. I loved those boys in that moment, and I knew that I would from that point on.

Then there was my family, who stood with me throughout the nightmare that was my reality. My brother and sister-in-law walked alongside me up the aisle to our place for the funeral Mass. I drew on their strength every step of the way and could not have proceeded without them. My nephew and nieces remained close by. Struggling with their own loss, they never lost sight of my needs. I know now that family can sustain you through the worst that life has to offer. They will always be there for me and me for them. We are part of each other's lives. A little bit of each of us died that day, and we clung to each other for strength.

I knew that I could not speak at Michael's funeral. There were moments when continuing to breathe was an effort. Yet I wanted to let the world know how much I loved this child. So I did what I always do; I wrote my words and had them printed as part of the Mass booklet. I would like to share those words with you.

My Dear Michael,

As I try to grapple with the reality of losing you on this earth, I am reminded of you as a small child, an abrasive teen, and a growing young man.

As a small child, your smile was the light of my life. When I held you in my arms, I felt certain that I was the luckiest woman alive. The Lord had chosen me to be your mom, and I was filled with gratitude. You were my son, and I was so proud.

As you grew, you presented challenges to me that were often beyond my strength, but someone was always there to help me be what you needed at the time. Though the years from teen to young adult were at times filled with frustration, anger, and fear, they never replaced the love we had, mine for you and yours in return.

In recent years, I was pleased to see the progress you were making—working hard to become a young man who could hold his head high and make a mother proud.

I was amazed at your mind; your level of thinking was beyond me. Your sense of humor was a joy and your creativity, a treasure. I always knew you were meant to be my child, though I never dreamt our time together would be so short. You taught me much in our time together. I am better because of you:

- ➤ *I have learned to be more patient instead of demanding that things be done in my time;*

- ➤ *I have learned to show more tolerance of others not like me;*

- ➤ *I have learned to enjoy laughter instead of taking myself so seriously;*

- ➤ *I have learned to love unconditionally, no matter what the cost; and*

- ➤ *I have learned to see each day as an opportunity to be more.*

I send you back now to the Lord from whom you came. You were His gift to me and now He wants you home.

All My Love

My last picture of Michael, age twenty-four

The next morning I woke up and stared at the ceiling, wondering how I would go on. This truly was the first day of the rest of my life, but I was not at all sure it was a life I wanted to live. The real grief began that Wednesday morning, and that is what I want this part of my message to convey. However, I felt that it was important to tell you at least a little about my Michael so that you could better understand the process of my grief. To know him was indeed to love him. How could anyone ignore his charm or that smile? However, I think it is also important for you to understand that to know him was to fear for him as well. He started life with such strikes against him, and ultimately that struggle took his young life. He evoked intense emotion in me and in most who knew him. He taught me that I was capable of a level of love I did not even know existed until I held him in my arms. He also taught me just how deeply I could feel anger and disappointment, anxiety and apprehension. He was a constant source of wonder to those around him. I was in awe of his talents and his intellect, yet grew tired of his antics and failures. I was continually afraid of the impact his behavior would have on his future. But above all else, I was his mother. I loved him no matter what, and that never changed. He was my son, and then he was gone.

While struggling through those years of raising my exceptional son alone, people would often ask me how I could continue to try one method after another, day after day. I was always puzzled by that question because it implied that there was a choice. I never felt that there was an option. He was my son, and I loved him more than life itself. The only option was to keep loving him and search for answers that would help him love himself.

10
The Early Days of Grief

No one ever told me that grief felt so like fear.
—C.S. Lewis

The only word that even begins to describe the early days after such a tragedy is numb. I felt numb for what seemed like a very long time. I would lie in bed early in the morning and try to muster the energy to get up. There didn't seem to be any reason to face another day of such intense pain. Sleep was really the only relief. At some point, something or someone would force me to get up and move through the day.

I don't remember even leaving the house for a long time. In part, my sense of exhaustion kept me home, but even more so was the fear. I had little control over my emotions, and I was terrified of facing other people, afraid to step into a world I felt I had left behind. Never in my life had I felt so frozen in one place, unable to move forward or back.

A good friend of mine was able to put my initial struggle into words; for a time, *grief owns you.* Those three simple words are a perfect description of the first few months after Michael's tragic death. I had no idea who I was anymore. I could not think clearly. The simplest tasks took all my energy; what reserves I once had were gone. The whole concept of time took on a new and unfamiliar meaning. I would find myself staring into space, certain that I had been sitting there for hours, only to discover that just a few minutes had passed.

Grief owns you, and you have no idea how to get yourself back. Where did the woman I once knew go? Thoughts continued to pop in and out of my head, yet I had no energy or ability to corral them. It was exhausting. Thankfully, this period of numbness eventually fades. I can't tell you how long it will last. I can't even tell you how long it lasted for me, because it's all such a blur. It's like being a visitor in your own life. It was a terrifying experience because I had no idea if it would ever end.

Eventually, I did venture out on my own. I knew it was critical to do so, and I promised myself I would on a particular day. I think it was a Tuesday, a few weeks after his funeral. I told myself that on Thursday I would go to the store. It was still two whole days away, so surely I could find the energy by then.

Thursday came, and I followed through with my promise. I made a list and drove to the local grocery store. I was walking the aisles, filling my cart, when suddenly items from the shelves started jumping out at me. Not literally, of course, but it seemed like they were larger than life—huge bottles of hot sauce, oversized boxes of Cream of Wheat, extra large Tombstone pizzas; all favorites of Michael's at various points in his life. I suddenly felt overwhelmed; the tears were streaming down my face. I wanted to scream; in fact, I was afraid that I *had* screamed. I left the cart, ran from the store, and drove home as fast as I could. I was so out of control that I scared myself. I just had to get home where I could hide.

I thank God that level of grief did not last. I was able to go through the motions of living soon after that experience. However, the loss of control did reappear many times with little or no notice. I remember taking his mountain bike to the local bike store to have it tuned up for my brother and sister-in-law. I knew how much they loved Michael, and that was the only thing of his that they wanted. I managed to get the bike into the trunk of my car and off I went. Once I arrived, I was not able to get the bike out on my own, so I went into the store and asked a young clerk if he could help me. We walked back into the store with the bike in tow, and there were two other customers looking for assistance. The young man began to write up the ticket for work on

Michael's bike. I stood there looking at the bright yellow bike, and I could almost see him sitting on top of it the day we bought it. Suddenly, I could not speak. I heard the clerk ask me what I wanted done on the bike, but I could not respond. I knew that if I so much as opened my mouth I would begin sobbing, so I just stood there. The other customers were becoming annoyed with me, but I was unable to respond to their need for me to get on with it. The clerk repeated his question several times, and though I was very uncomfortable, I just stared at him and at the bike. Finally, the moment passed, and I was able to conclude my business. No one else in that store had any idea what I was going through in those moments, but I had no choice but to allow the feelings to pass through me so I could continue.

I learned a vital lesson that afternoon. The sense of grief and the loss of control that accompanies death will surface whenever they choose. I knew it was unhealthy for me to try to stifle such intense emotion. I also realized that it would pass through on its own, and I would once again be able to appear to function normally. The key for me was not to try to control it, but allow it to surface and fade as a natural part of the painful process of grief.

The denial that is part of grief manifested itself in a number of ways, some more overt than others. I remember returning home many times, opening the door from the garage to the kitchen, and actually expecting to hear "Hi, Mom." As I lay in bed late at night, I swore I could hear the garage door opening. A couple of times, the experience was so real that I actually got up and checked to make sure he had not arrived home, as had happened so many nights before. Our minds play cruel and vivid tricks on us throughout the process of grief. Because grief owns you, it's in charge. In retrospect, I think it's God's way of gently bringing us to the point that we can accept the finality of death as a reality. The frequency of such mind tricks lessened over time as I began to face the awful truth that death is forever.

I have no idea if the grief process I am experiencing is similar for others, though I am quite sure that it is not exactly the same for everyone. I describe it here in the hope that there may be some similarities, and my experiences may provide a sense of hope for others experiencing such grief. The intensity involved is so foreign to us that it is impossible to know what is "normal." It is frightening to be so out of control and not know if the condition will ever change. I can tell you with certainty that it does change, I simply cannot tell you when or how. Eventually, with help, we move through these stages. It's important to know that we'll never be the same as we were before. The death of a child changes you. As time and the process continue, you begin to realize that you are changing. It's impossible not to, because a part of you has died. How successfully you navigate the grief process will determine in part who you become. The journey is scary because it is filled with unknowns. Faith becomes a more critical component of your life than it ever was before. I was frequently aware that I felt like a child of God and because of my faith, I knew I would survive. I just had no idea who I was becoming.

My recollection of those early days is not very clear. I suspect that is partly because my head was not very clear. I think I just moved from one day to the next. I do remember feeling like time was moving unnaturally slowly. Ten and fifteen minute increments often seemed like hours. I would look at the clock often, hoping the day was passing quickly, only to discover that it had only been a few minutes since my last glance at the clock. I'm reminded here of all the clichés we hear at a time like this—"Just stay busy," "Put one foot in front of the other," "Take it one day at a time," and so on. There is actually truth to those words.

I was retired by the time Michael died, so I was not able to "stay busy" with work, which was both a blessing and a curse. I do remember making it through one day, and then telling myself I just had to make it through one more. Eventually, the days passed, and each hour did not seem so unnaturally long. In the beginning, it is, I think, a matter of just getting by. Sometimes all I could focus on was breathing. Other times I was able to be with others and actually appear to be enjoying myself. One day after another becomes months, and eventually years, and you realize that you are making it, sometimes in spite of yourself. *Grief owns you* for a time, and it is very reluctant to release its grip on your heart. I do not believe it ever really leaves, but little by little you regain a measure of control over yourself and your life.

11
<u>All the Firsts</u>

Grief is the price we pay for love.

—Elizabeth II

As I indicated earlier, I am a person of deep faith, and for years I tried to nurture such faith in my son. I brought him to church, taught him prayers before meals and bed, and encouraged him to rely on God's love for him. As the years went on, this effort became more difficult, in part because of Michael's behavior. The Catholic Church, to which I have belonged my entire adult life, was not a comfortable place for my son to be. He was not allowed to attend religious education classes because his behavior was disruptive. While I understood their concern for other children in the classes, I was confused by the church's lack of alternatives for children with special needs. No additional assistance was ever offered, and so I struggled alone. Eventually, it became clear that Michael would never completely embrace the church of my childhood. Therefore, I concentrated on teaching him through my example as best I could.

Over the years, my frustration with the Catholic Church grew. I found no comfort or assistance through the organized church and instead began to rely more on my own personal relationship with God as a means of guidance and strength. As a result, my son grew up without the structure of an organized church for support. My attempts to teach by example only went so far and seemed completely ignored throughout his teen years. The more I professed a deep faith in a loving God, the more Michael voiced a lack of belief in any god. I prayed long and hard that he would feel the presence of God in his life and in his heart. At times, I noticed with great relief that his anti-religious words often did not match his actions. He understood the values I tried to instill in him, and those values showed despite his desire to rebel. So I simply continued to quietly pray. Then he died.

While my church was not helpful in my attempts to instill a sense of faith in my son, I didn't know where else to turn when he died. So I called my local church to set up funeral arrangements. I remember that appointment like it was yesterday. A good friend accompanied me, in part because I didn't know what to expect. I knew I was not a solid member of the congregation in their eyes, but I prayed that the church authorities would accept me and my son, and help me through this painful process. A nun who worked in the parish greeted us. I braced myself for her criticism of my lack of involvement in church-related activities, because sadly, that had been my experience with many Catholic religious leaders. However, her initial words took my breath away. She looked at me kindly and said, "Tell me about your son." I will never forget her compassion that day. I remember that I just started talking about Michael. I told her of his struggles and his talents. I related stories of his antics and accomplishments. I showed her pictures of him at various points in his life. I just couldn't seem to stop talking about him. She never rushed me. She never looked like she was getting tired of listening. She never knew this young man, but she succeeded in convincing me that she wanted to. She helped me plan a service that was right for him, and I was so very grateful. That was perhaps the first time I realized how vitally important it is to keep talking about Michael. I never tire of telling "Michael stories," and I am blessed with many people in my life who never seem to tire of listening.

I chose passages to read and songs to sing. I busied myself with thoughts about who I would ask to participate in each facet of the service. The funeral itself was comforting and beautiful, if such a painful experience can be described in those terms. The priest didn't know Michael either, and he didn't try to sound like he did. Rather, he faced the congregation and announced that he had not known this young man, and then he invited others who did to come forward and speak of him.

I had been distant from my church for many years, but that day I felt like I had come home and my son was welcome at last.

In those first weeks after his death, I prayed for a sign that my son was in heaven. I believe strongly in an afterlife, one that invites us to enjoy the love and companionship of our Father for all eternity. I desperately needed to know that my son had found such peace, and so I prayed for a sign. I was very clear with God in those first shaky weeks. I needed a clear sign, nothing vague or ambiguous. I needed a strong, definitive sign that I could not possibly overlook or misunderstand.

As time went on, I continued to pay close attention to my own needs and worked hard to seek the support necessary to move through the grief process. I became aware that I needed to get away and spend some time alone. I went to the Arizona desert for a couple of weeks to reflect on how the loss of my son had changed my life and me forever. Who was I now, and why was I here? What was my purpose in life now that he was gone? It was almost six months after his death, and I needed the time alone to pray for the strength to continue living. In retrospect, I can see how healing those days were for me. I spent my time soaking up the warmth of the sun and reading material that I hoped would help me understand the grief I was living. During that time, I continued to pray for a sign that my son was at peace and enjoying all the benefits of eternal life. I had no idea what form such a sign would take, but I knew it would come, and I would know when it arrived.

It was mid-October when I returned home. The weather in the Midwest was turning toward winter. The trees were shedding their leaves, the air was crisp and cold, and the flowers in the gardens were gone. In the courtyard in front of my home, I have a rose bush that has been there for several years. Every season the bush would yield one stalk that grew about three feet tall and blossomed into one large and beautiful salmon-colored rose. I tried various techniques to encourage the bush to become fuller, but nothing helped. No matter what I did, each year I would get one stalk and one rose.

When I returned home from Arizona, I noticed that the rose bush was growing another stem, one that seemed taller than any that had preceded it. I remember thinking that this was odd, given the time of year, but I chalked it up to the fact that this particular bush had always been a little strange. During the next couple of weeks, the stem continued to grow tall and straight toward the sky. It was simply one thin stem rapidly growing taller each day. It looked so strange, and reminded me of the "beanstalk" in the fairytale I learned as a child. One day I noticed a bud at the very tip of the stalk. By this time, the weather was quite cold, and the bud looked frozen, perched on top of the long, thin stem.

Some very good friends of mine had purchased a beautiful memorial tree to plant in Michael's honor in a park near our home. Six months after his death, the tree was scheduled to be planted, and a memorial service was planned for November 1. That morning, I opened my front door to take out the dog and was stunned to see that a large, beautiful, salmon-colored rose had blossomed overnight at the very tip of the tall rose stem. The flower was alive and growing, despite the fact that we had already experienced several days of below-freezing temperatures. All the other plants in my garden had gone into hibernation for the winter, but there was this beautiful blooming rose. I was overwhelmed. This had to be the sign for which I prayed—I have always loved flowers and routinely spend much time and money on my gardens; Michael often teased me about this passion. Flowers do not bloom in November in Chicago, I told myself. This particular bush had never grown taller than three feet, yet here it was over six feet tall. Michael was six foot three inches, an inch or two taller than this beautiful sign, and I rejoiced that morning in the knowledge that he was in heaven. Several hours later, I realized that this message was also from my mother, who had died eight years earlier. She understood my grief deeply, as she too had lost a child, my sister Susan, who died at the age of twenty-nine, more than thirty years ago. My mother's name was Rose.

Courtyard Rose

I knew my child was in heaven with my mom. I immediately felt a sense of peace that I had not felt since he died. The grief continued, but my fears were gone. I knew he was in the hands of a loving God; I no longer had to worry about his care.

The end of that first year was very difficult. I was facing the holidays without my son. I really didn't know what to expect, but I paid close attention to the advice of those who loved me, and all of them told me not to put unnecessary pressure on myself. All of those first big holidays—Thanksgiving, Christmas, and New Year's—were incredibly painful. I felt like I vacillated between numbness and tears.

My extended family is quite small. I have only one brother, and he and his wife live nearby with their three children, all of whom made a special point to care for me that first year. We always spend a fun and casual Christmas Eve at my house, and then have a wonderful dinner at my brother's on Christmas day. I was not at all sure how I was going to handle it, but I was determined that our traditions not be altered. I needed the comfort of familiarity—at least as far as that was possible without Michael.

Although it may seem odd to say so, that first Christmas Eve was a true blessing for me. For many years, my family has been joined by very good friends on that evening, and we always have a wonderful time together. In addition, that first Christmas Eve brought a special gift—five of Michael's friends spent the evening with us. To this day, I'm not sure if they came because they needed to remember him on that day or they were simply demonstrating a kind affection toward me, and it really doesn't matter. All I know is that the gift of their presence was a treasure. We ate and drank; we laughed and cried. We played games until the early morning hours, and somehow they got me through that first dreaded Christmas Eve. I will forever remember their kindness that night. These young men had carried my son to his grave earlier that year, and they were with me to remember him. We laughed and cried together that day, remembering the Michael we all knew and loved.

My sister-in-law had made prior arrangements to have me return to their home that night because she did not want me to awaken that first Christmas morning alone. Though I have always maintained an independent spirit, I allowed myself to be guided through those first holidays, responding as best I could to the tender loving care my family and friends offered. I doubt that I would have made it through those days without all the kindness they showered on me.

I suspect that this was the second significant lesson I learned in this process—the importance of allowing others to care for you. Not only was it impossible for me to be myself through that first holiday season, it was critical to my family that they be allowed to step in and care for me. They loved Michael, too. They had lost an integral part of their family circle, and in their own way, they were grieving that loss. They needed to help, and my job was to let them.

Christmas morning came quickly, and I awoke feeling drained. My sister-in-law spent a good part of the day preparing a spectacular dinner. We all exchanged gifts, as is our tradition. Then there was a moment in the day that will remain with me forever. My brother is not one to speak easily of the kind of emotion that goes with experiencing such a tragedy. As a result, he rarely spoke to me at all of Michael or the pain he felt in losing him. My brother is one who shows his love through actions rather than words. While I knew Michael's death had a profound impact on him, it was a rare thing to be able to share a conversation like that with him and even more rare to be able to cry together.

On that first Christmas, when all the gifts were opened and all the boxes and papers cleared away, my brother walked toward me and announced that they had one more gift for me. He choked back tears as he tried to speak, and yet he seemed determined to be the one to extend this final gift. He and his family had made a charitable donation in Michael's name because they wanted to make sure that Michael was remembered that Christmas day. As he got the words out and handed me the envelope, he put his arm around me, and for the first time since Michael died, we held each other and cried together, knowing how painful this loss was to each of us. I know how hard it was for my brother to do that, and I know he did it for me. I think of that moment often, and I thank God for his love. We will always be there for each other, no matter what. Our parents and our sister died many years ago. We are all that is left of the family we grew up with, and we both know that nothing will ever come between us. That day, my brother's gift was not only the donation remembering Michael, it was also the glimpse he offered at the pain that he too will always carry now that Michael is gone. A pain that stems from the love he feels for Michael and the sadness he feels to see me in such pain.

The first News Year's Eve was another in a series of surprises for me. For a long time, I had been part of a delightful tradition that begins late in the afternoon on New Year's Eve day. My brother and his college friend scour the area for various dinner delicacies. They travel to many restaurants picking up orders for special appetizers and dinner items. They invite all the women in their lives to meet for a special celebration.

This includes their mothers-in-law, their wives, their daughters, and even their sisters. Then for the entire evening, up to the stroke of midnight, they serve us special drinks and a lavish, delicious meal. We bring in the New Year together, celebrating the special bond of family and friends. I have always looked forward to this traditional event. It is a spectacular gathering for all involved.

However, that first year, New Year's Eve was extremely painful for me. I tried so very hard to celebrate with the others, but I felt no such sense of joy. The new year just meant a full year without Michael, and that emptiness was pervasive to me. Because all the guests involved love me, they understood my pain and allowed me to be myself. They showed a surprising ability to nurture me in my sadness without diminishing their joy. They were all a gift to me that year, and I will not soon forget their compassion.

I should mention here that over time, I have discovered that New Year's Eve remains the hardest day of the year for me. I am not sure why, perhaps it's just the awareness of another year on the horizon without my Michael. Perhaps it's the stark contrast of my sadness in the midst of such joyous celebration. I have learned to accept this reality for me. I am gentle with myself on that day. I expect very little, and I allow myself to experience whatever feelings arise in me. I have come to realize that it is that willingness to accept rather than fight that has allowed me to move forward through the healing process. I encourage anyone who grieves the loss of their child to recognize that feeling of acceptance and embrace it, for it is the means to a healthy sense of healing from the most devastating of events.

I know there are well-defined stages of grief, and I tried in those early months to read everything I could get my hands on that might shed some light on what was happening to me. I did not find anything that was very helpful, probably because my mind could not hold the words. I would read, read, and reread again, but nothing stuck. It was too soon. I was not ready to absorb information. I needed most of my energy each day just to survive. I was blessed with two good friends who had also lost children several years earlier. Each of them very lovingly told me over and over again to follow my instinct, don't push myself to be more than I could be, take each day as it comes, and most importantly, always be kind to myself. It was good advice, and I followed their lead.

The process of grief floods you with intense emotions. One of the most difficult to manage is anger. The entire emotional cycle is erratic. You may vacillate between anger and sorrow to numbness and anxiety and back again in the span of a few minutes. Each emotion has its own path; some are short, some are not. In the initial stages of grief, you never know the duration, you may not understand the immediate cause, and the intensity is often frightening. However, because the feelings are so strong, you really have no choice but to move through them, no matter the circumstances.

I was very angry that my son died. At times, I still feel the anger, but the intensity has diminished. I was angry with him because the circumstances of his death could have been avoided. He was showing off a gun he had purchased while he was drinking. Those two things should never occur together. I kept asking myself, "He knew better, didn't he? Why did he feel such a need to show off?" I hate guns of any kind, and I always have. I worked my entire career in the juvenile justice system and saw firsthand the tragedy that guns can cause in the hands of teenagers or in the hands of adults who think like adolescents. That pretty much describes my son. In some ways he had been maturing into a responsible adult, but in many ways he still acted like an impulsive teen, and that weakness resulted in his untimely death.

Yes, I was angry. Many a night I sat thinking of his final moments, and my mind would scream, "Didn't I tell you guns were dangerous?" How could he have been so irresponsible? In my calmer moments, I can answer that question. In many ways, that was very much like Michael. He was irresponsible. Rarely did he think of consequences before he acted. Finally, his actions were severe enough that they resulted in his death.

Sometimes the anger is misdirected. It can be hard to be angry at the person who died; after all, they paid the ultimate price. So your anger manifests itself in other ways. Sometimes, on the road, I felt so angry with other drivers that it scared me. A couple of times I just went home, changing my plans on the spot because I didn't trust myself to continue. Once again, I tried to follow the advice of my friends, and I paid attention to myself and my own limitations.

It is also easy to get angry at those around you, especially those with whom you are most secure. I am not married, so in my case there was no spouse upon whom to dump my anger. I'm sure that often happens with parents who lose a child. It's so easy to direct the anger at your partner, especially if their manner of grieving is different than your own. I never had that option, but my anger was often misdirected at my remaining family. I got mad at my nieces and nephew or I often lost my temper with my brother or sister-in-law. How could they not know this or that? How could they just go back to their lives as if nothing had happened? How could they laugh and seem so happy? Didn't they love Michael too? Why weren't they sad that he was gone? Why didn't they talk about him anymore?

Finally, I directed my anger at God. I always had a strong faith, but now, when I needed it most, my faith was weakened. How could a loving God have allowed this to happen? Where was He when my beautiful son needed Him the most? He, more than anyone, knew how much Michael had struggled throughout his life. What was the point of all of that hardship? It just didn't seem fair, and the truth is, it wasn't fair. Much of life isn't fair; much is hard to understand. I guess that is the whole point of faith.

Gratefully, after a while, the anger subsided. God was gentle with me and allowed me to come to my own conclusions eventually. The truth is that God did not cause this tragedy to happen. It was in fact an accident, caused by Michael's own choices. We must all live with the choices we make in this life, and sometimes we die as a result of those choices. I still feel anger from time to time, but now, when it surfaces, it's directed at Michael. It doesn't last but a few moments because I can't stay angry at the child I raised. There is too much love there for the anger to remain.

More often than not I tried to hide the anger I felt. This was especially true with the intensity of feelings directed toward my extended family. I grew up in a house with eight people, parents, siblings, grandparents, and one cousin. My brother and I are the only ones left now, and he and I have grown closer over the years. He married a wonderful woman who has become much more like a sister to me than an in-law. She and I have become close friends. They have three children whom I have loved since their births. I feel blessed to have had the opportunity to play such an important role in their lives. We all lived close together, and as a result, their kids and my son grew up together. I know that each of them grieve the loss of Michael, but I also know that their way of showing that struggle is different than mine.

This reality was difficult and painful for me to understand. They rarely speak of Michael, and some are visibly uncomfortable when I do. Many times in the last couple of years, I have struggled to hide the anger I felt because some part of me knew that the anger was not really directed at them. I watched them move on with their lives. They went to school, secured good jobs, got married, bought cars and houses, and generally enjoyed their successful passage into adulthood. I was happy for them, but that happiness was always touched with regret. The joy I felt when they experienced success was always a bit marred by sadness. How could I tell them how I really felt? I worked hard at not showing the sense of emptiness that often accompanied my pride in their accomplishments. At times, it was exhausting.

Feeling such opposite emotions simultaneously is confusing at best, but I have come to understand that it is a necessary part of my grief. How could I not be sad and envious? How could I not regret that my son will never meet the love of his life? It is a natural part of the process, and to deny such emotions only prolongs the pain. I know my family will understand my ambivalence because I know they love me, and more importantly, they loved Michael. They too feel the mixed emotion that his absence creates. It took me a very long time to understand this and really believe it, because they so rarely speak of him anymore. But when they do, the emotion is right there, no matter how much time has passed. I have learned to relish those moments when they come because they are truly a gift, one that, though rare, is treasured.

On the first anniversary of Michael's death, we had the first "Remember Michael Party." My brother and his wife hosted it at my request, and my family and close friends attended. In addition, several of Michael's friends wanted to spend the evening with us, and I was thrilled. We spent the evening together eating, drinking, laughing and crying. We all told Michael stories, and I delighted in listening to others speak of my son. At one point, one of Mike's friends asked me exactly what had happened that dreadful night, a year earlier. I realized that some of them didn't know the specifics of how he died, and they too deserved to know the truth. I described in detail everything I knew about his death that night, and his friends cried as I spoke.

We spent several hours together that evening. I even remember feeling that some of their Michael stories were more than a mother needs to hear. There is definitely a reason why our children do not tell us everything about their lives away from our protective care. But I was thrilled to be in the company of his friends, and so I listened and laughed as they related stories involving careless driving escapades, underage drinking experiences, and a variety of "close calls" of one kind or another.

As the night ended, several of his friends mentioned that they wanted to do this every year on or around the anniversary of his death. We all promised to get together the first weekend in May the following year. I was touched by their desire to continue to share their lives with me, and to do so near the anniversary of Michael's death was the only way they could include him in the festivities. However, I never really believed that it would continue. Rather, I remember just being grateful for that first time together, and I loved every one of them for caring enough to make that effort.

12
The Hardest Year

Everyone can master grief but he that has it.
—William Shakespeare

In some ways, I think the second year after the loss of a child is even more difficult than the first. During most of the first year, you are painfully aware of the erratic nature of the emotions that such a tragedy creates in you. Others around you are often aware of that too. Friends and family are very attuned to your needs, and they watch over you and protect you whenever possible.

To quote poet Robert Frost (1875–1963), "In three words I can sum up everything I've learned about life. It goes on." Life goes on, and for others it may go on before you are ready to climb aboard. As the months and years go by, friends stop calling to see how you are. There are fewer and fewer cards and notes in the mail just to let you know that someone is thinking about you. Fewer and fewer people even mention your child's name, almost as if he never existed. I felt all of those things as I moved through the second year after Michael's death. The sense of loneliness was harsh. I knew in no uncertain terms that, no matter what I might have thought, I was totally alone in this grief. I guess that makes sense when you think about it.

No one felt the loss of this person as I did. How could I have even thought they might? The rest of the world moved on with life as usual. I was the only one who no longer had a usual path for life to travel. I know now that the kind of loneliness I am describing occurs at some point to any parent who has lost a child. It is like standing on the sidelines while the merry-go-round continues to rotate with everyone else you love still aboard. Occasionally you have the energy to hop on, and for a moment, life seems normal again. Then you remember, and as you do, you find yourself standing still while the world rotates around you.

Will it always be this way? I'm not sure, because "always" is a very long time. That is one of the things that has changed about me. I'm no longer certain of many things. Time is both a friend and an enemy to grief. The passage of time does help you to rejoin others in the life that is before you. However, the simple fact that time can be measured also demonstrates how far removed you are from life as you knew it. It's like becoming a watch that no longer keeps accurate time and has to be repeatedly reset. Each time you look you are surprised at how far off you are from those around you.

The second year of grief is therefore one of loneliness. Allow yourself to be alone and feel alone. It is not so frightening after a while. It's an important step in the process, because it's the beginning of getting to know who you are becoming. If, during this time, you find a friend or two who will still listen to your pain, rejoice. I have been lucky enough to find such friends. I used journaling as a means of coping with the intense feelings that persisted during a time when the world seemed to be telling me that I should be better by now. I routinely e-mailed my thoughts to my loving friends, and each one responded with kind, compassionate understanding every time I reached out. What a treasured gift they were to me. Yet I learned to be careful about who I included in those writings. While I'm blessed with many friends, I quickly discovered that some were better able to handle the intensity of my pain.

There were the friends who wanted to try to "fix" things so that the hurt would not be so raw. I knew there was no "fix" to be had. But I learned that for some, my speaking honestly about it caused them pain because they desperately needed to find a solution.

Some were just frightened by my words. They would call almost immediately after reading my thoughts, and I could hear the fear in their voices. They must have thought I was on the verge of taking my own life. They did not understand that in fact "life" as I knew it had already died.

Mostly I wrote late at night when the loneliness I felt was so evident. I would sit at my computer and pour out my heart to those few friends who I knew would understand and not judge. The tears always came as the words flowed. Many nights I sobbed as I wrote about the extent of the pain that seemed overwhelming. In the process, a miraculous thing happened. As the words poured out of me, so did the feelings, and by the time I was finished, I felt a sense of peace. In the end, I was exhausted, but free to sleep through the night and awaken with the strength to face another day. Invariably in the morning, there would be responses from my friends. Responses filled with kind words, compassionate thoughts, and a loving invitation to continue to use them as my sounding board.

Those friends helped me to move through the loneliness to the point where I could face the person I was becoming without fear. They each gave me so much, and I hope they know how grateful I am. I would not be me without their loving friendship, and I will cherish them for their gift until the day that I die.

13
As Time Moves On

Death leaves a heartache no one can heal,
love leaves a memory no one can steal.
                    —From a headstone in Ireland

The image set forth by the word "celebrate" may seem totally out of place to many who are grieving, but I think not. I really do believe in celebrating my son's life, even though at times that concept is difficult for even me to grasp. Michael was a living, breathing young man with talents and faults, and I must continue to celebrate the time we had together, because that time is precious to me, now more than ever.

As I am writing this chapter, I have just survived the second anniversary of his death. That date came just one day before Mother's Day this year, so it was a rather pensive and sad weekend. But just one short week later, the celebration began.

About six weeks ago, I received a phone call from one of Michael's closest friends. Bryan is a newly married young man who recently purchased his first home in a nearby community. He was calling because he said it was time for the "Remember Michael" party. As I described earlier, Mike's friends had gathered with my family and friends to remember him on the first anniversary of his death. Several of the young people there told me they wanted to get together each year at this time, and I encouraged them to do so. I never really believed that they would continue this tradition. Each of them has a life of his own with exciting new experiences ahead. They are getting engaged and married, moving forward in their chosen careers, and buying first homes—it was a naturally self-absorbed time in their young lives. I know they miss Mike, but I never really believed that two years later they would make such an effort to remember him.

Therefore, the call came as both a surprise and a delight. They did remember, and they wanted to get together again to tell Michael stories and celebrate the life of the one we all lost that day in May two years earlier. Bryan wanted to have the party at his house, a chance to show off his new home, and I was thrilled. There were fifteen to twenty people there, and we had a wonderful time. These young people, less than half my age, taught me a great many things. They knew my son in a different way than I did, and I delighted in getting to know him better through their eyes. Their loyalty to his memory has taught me about the depth of their friendship, something I wholeheartedly value. My friends have helped me to survive this loss, and I thank God daily for their support. I tried hard, through both words and example, to teach my son about the precious value of friendship. Now I know he listened. What a gift!

We spent several hours together, eating, drinking, and enjoying each other's company. It was as if part of Michael was there, a little piece of him in each of us. I could almost see him in their gestures and hear him in their laughter. It was so clear that they loved their friend and that they miss him when they are together. Several times throughout the afternoon and evening, I just sat back and watched them. I am proud of these young men and women. They truly understand the importance of what they lost, a lesson many older adults never seem to comprehend. The pain of their loss has changed them too, as it has changed me. They treasure their time together, because they understand it is not guaranteed. They carried their friend to his grave, and they are not about to forget the lessons his death taught them. They are much more aware of what is important in life, and they are young enough to take full advantage of that insight.

Though Michael's death was a very painful loss for all of them, it was a kind of wake-up call. Each of them understands that time is not infinite, and they must make the most of what they have. He left them a gift, and they are putting it to good use. Michael would be proud of his friends, and he understands what a gift they are to me!

Certainly, it is true that these celebrations do not come without a price. Throughout the evening, it is painfully clear to me that, while their lives are becoming more exciting, Michael's ended before it ever really began. This makes the emptiness inside me feel even larger when matched against the fullness of their lives. Yet, feeling that pain is well worth it to me, because it allows me to be in the company of others who cared deeply about my son, and that experience is more important that words can convey

That is probably the greatest fear of any bereaved parent, that his or her child will be forgotten. When death comes to someone after a long and productive life, there was an opportunity for many people to have been touched by that life, and that person is unlikely to be forgotten. But that is not the case with a child or even a young adult just beginning to branch out into the world. Michael was my only immediate family, and I am frequently overwhelmed by the fear that when I am gone, the memory of him will go with me.

Such a fear poses questions about the purpose of life. I believe that my son's life had purpose, but I must also admit that I don't know what that purpose was. I make guesses in my mind, mostly to bring a sense of peace and finality to my questions, but the truth is, I don't really know. That's one of the reasons these annual gatherings are so important. I feel blessed with the opportunity to see firsthand that Michael touched many lives beyond mine. This awareness makes it easy for me to believe that his life has had an impact beyond what I originally imagined. He must have been a very good friend to the young people gathered before me, and through them, he will go on to touch the lives of others in ways I can't even imagine.

So I will continue to tell Michael stories and encourage others to do the same. The telling of such stories is part of the process of healing. Every time I hear someone else use his name, I feel a warmth in my heart. Other people also loved my son, and they too miss him. What a gift their stories are to me. I long for the day when my brother and all his children freely speak of the Michael they knew so well. I continue to hope that day will come, and when it does, I will experience true joy once again.

The sadness you feel when you lose a child never really goes away. I assume that is true because it has only been a few years for me, and "never" is a very long time. However, I think it's safe to say that the sadness lingers. It's not as prevalent as it was in the early months or even throughout the first year, but it's there. It takes over suddenly, and with an intensity that continues to surprise me.

For example, I am sad today. It's a week before the anniversary of my son's death, and generally speaking, life is going pretty well for me. It looks like a beautiful spring is on the horizon, the flowering trees are in bloom, and soon the gardens will be full of beautiful flowers. I just had my living space painted, and the result has enabled me to fall in love with my home all over again. In a few days, I will be going away with friends for some fun and relaxation, but the truth is, I feel terribly sad today. The tears are right behind my eyelids, and my whole body feels sad.

I was invited to go to a long-anticipated party tonight. Friends are celebrating the safe return of their young son from the war in Iraq. We have all worried about Brian and continually prayed for his safe return. He has come home now, and I can't think of a better reason for a celebration, but I can't go. I have come to the point in my grief where I can gauge the intensity of my sadness, and I know I can't hide it tonight. My son will never come home again, and I feel so cheated. Brian and his family deserve to be happy; I can only imagine the relief they must feel. All I know for sure is that they do not need to feel sad tonight, and sadness is all I have to give.

So I will stay home and allow the sadness to move through me, just like the anger that came before it. I have never been very successful at controlling these emotions, and I know I allow them to control me at times. The best I can do is not inflict them on others when to do so could cause harm. There will be other days when I can celebrate with friends and family, and I have learned to appreciate those times more than ever. For now, I will stay home, because the sadness has to have a place to go. I know it will not stay long, but I have learned to respect it while it is here. The depth of my sadness is in a way the measure of my love for Michael, and that is something I cannot hide. The absence his death has created is with me always, and sometimes that emptiness comes to the surface whether I want it to or not. The love is still there; it just has no child to hug.

The beauty of time, though, is that now I know this too will pass. I'm no longer afraid that I will feel nothing but sadness because I have also felt joy. A young man whom I care about is safely home tonight with his family and friends, and that is something well worth celebrating. It is indeed a joyous occasion, joyous enough to demand that I stay home.

14
Stages

Tearless grief bleeds inwardly.

—Christian Novell Bovee

There are many books out there on the subject of grief. I certainly don't claim to be an authority or even well read on the subject. Nevertheless, I thought it was important to review some of the information available as a means of better understanding what was happening to me.

Like all students in the field of psychology, I was somewhat familiar with the early works of Dr. Elisabeth Kubler-Ross, a compassionate pioneer in the field of bereavement theory. However, I must also admit that I don't recall much detail from her work or the writings of other authors on the subject of grief. I am somewhat familiar with what Dr. Kubler-Ross delineates as the five stages of grief, also known as the "grief cycle." Attempts to organize the process of grief is a common theme used by many writers on the subject. Regardless of what a particular author calls them, the stages form what I think of as a framework that can lead to a better understanding of grief and all its complexities.

As I tried to compare what was happening to me with any of the theoretical concepts I remembered, I became aware that the process was far from sequential. Kubler-Ross was clear about that fact, but I so wanted the cycle to be orderly. Grief is anything but. It would have been so much easier if only I could tell where I was in the process and what was coming next. That never happened for me.

The stages according to Dr. Kubler-Ross are:

➢ Denial
➢ Anger
➢ Bargaining
➢ Depression
➢ Acceptance

Others use such terms like:

➢ Numbness
➢ Yearning
➢ Despair
➢ Reorganization
➢ Letting Go

Or

➢ Shock
➢ Suffering
➢ Recovery

I really didn't care what the stages were called, I just wanted there to be an order to them, a sequential order. I needed to know that I was progressing. Because the process of grief is so emotionally intense, it often results in an overwhelming sense of fear. You wonder if you will ever be the same again. There is no way of knowing the answer to that question, because while in the throes of grief, you do not even recognize yourself. That is exactly why I searched for a sense of order.

Instead, I found myself bouncing back and forth through the most intense emotions I had ever experienced. One day I would feel pervasively sad, and then I would wake the next morning trying to convince myself that this tragedy was not real. I just knew he would show up again; he would walk through that door and this nightmare would finally be over. When the denial faded, the exhaustion and numbness reappeared.

The point here is that there is no order, no linear progression to the chaos. While going through the process, you never know what "the end" will feel like. Perhaps you reach a point where you feel you are pulling your life back together, and then a day comes in which you find yourself unable to follow through with even the simplest tasks. Your mind races from one incoherent thought to another, and you realize that you are moving backward. It can be terrifying.

While there certainly were negative aspects to the fact that I was forced to go through this process alone, I also am aware of the benefits such solitude provided. I imagine that the process is often even more difficult when two parents are suffering, each in their own individual way. I suspect that the differences each parent displays can result in serious conflict. Perhaps one is moving along faster or in a seemingly healthier manner than the other. Watching your spouse bounce through the various stages in a different way or at a different pace than you must result in tremendous pain. It is no wonder that marriages often experience severe stress upon the death of a child.

I never had to cope with the differences between my grief and that of a spouse. My struggle related solely to feeling completely alone. No one was experiencing the loss of Michael quite as I was. I was his only parent, and no one loved him more. The darkness that invades your life at such a time simply adds to the fear and sense of disorder. As the months and years pass by, you continue to search for an end to the pain. Then one day you realize that there is no end, and there never will be. In my opinion, that is the beginning of real healing.

After several years, talking about Michael still often brings me to tears. Is that really so surprising? Does that mean I'm not making progress? I think not. Rather, I believe that I will always feel emotional when I think of him, when I speak of him, when I thumb through old photos of him. How could I think that would ever end? My love for him did not die. I don't miss him less this year than I did last. Because my love for my child is a forever thing, the tears will always be too. I think it's a form of courage to take the risk to show the world that you still love and miss your child. Perhaps your way is different than mine. I have always been a talker, thus it's no surprise that my way is to speak of him and listen to others speak of him. The tears still come; I no longer even try to control them. In a way, I am proud of my tears, because for me they show how much I loved him and that my deep sense of loss at his death has become a permanent part of me.

Learning to live with that day in and day out is the real definition of healing. It does not mean that the hurt will disappear or that the pain will subside completely. I know now that will never happen. The pain is with me from now on, and sometimes I cry, but I also can laugh. Sometimes I feel sad, but I have also known joy. I am progressing, but now I understand that there will be no end to this journey.

15
Helping Others to Help You

There is no grief like the grief that does not speak.
—Henry Wadsworth Longfellow

While immersed in the various stages of grief, it was virtually impossible for me to be clear about what I needed. I had never experienced anything close to the emotional intensity involved, and it took all my energy to simply put one foot in front of the other each day. There was no way to know what tomorrow would bring or how to prepare for it. My sense of time wavered with each day. How can you possibly know what you need now or what you may need later when you cannot even understand what's happening to you? The sense of fear is so pervasive that survival is your constant focus. Your only thought is *How am I going to get through this day?* It's certainly no wonder that it's not possible to identify and express your needs.

The day does come, though, when life returns to some semblance of normal. It is not a sudden shift, but rather a gradual movement from chaos to order. You realize one day that you are once again able to make a list of needed groceries and follow through with their purchase. You remember that the car needs an oil change and take care of it as you have so many times in the past. Life begins again to move in somewhat of a normal cycle, where an hour actually feels like an hour again and not a day. You find yourself returning to the routine in which you previously found some comfort. The needs are still there, but they no longer seem solely related to survival. Even in the midst of such extreme discomfort, time does have a positive effect. I hesitate to say it "heals" because I don't believe real and complete healing from such grief ever occurs. The term implies a progression toward an end, and I believe that the grief experienced with the death of a child never fully ends. It simply becomes a part of you, and you learn to live with it.

This is the point at which you are able to express your needs. You can verbalize to family and friends exactly what you wish them to do and say (or not do and say). Throughout this process, we all experience people saying and doing the "wrong" things. You may hear "you just need to stay busy" in response to your continued tears. Maybe someone close to you makes it a point to never mention your child's name because he or she is sure it will make you sad. The truth is that the sadness is forever present. It never goes away. More to the point, hearing someone else remember your child brings a warmth to your heart that accompanies the sadness. It makes you feel less alone.

I think it's important to tell those we love exactly what we need. Although we may not always know what that is or how to express it, we do know how it feels when someone says or does the "right" thing. That's when we need to speak and tell people how much we appreciate what they do or say, that we wish they would say it or do it more often, because it reminds us that others loved and miss our children. Having people around us who are not afraid to take this risk is such a gift. I believe that gift should be cherished.

As the years since my son's death move on, I find myself continuing to tell "Michael stories," but each time I have to fight the tendency to deny myself this luxury. Thoughts flash through my mind announcing that his death was too long ago or that I told this story before. I try each time to ignore the negative thoughts and relate the story that I know I have voiced many times to many people over the span of the last six years. I am blessed with many friends and family who laugh each time they hear the same story repeated. They seem to just know that my need to tell it is important. How else can I keep the spirit of my son alive in the life I now live without him? For those of you who may not be as blessed as I, I urge you to tell those you love how important it is for you to speak of your child, and how much you yearn for them to do the same.

The death of a child is, of course, against the natural order of things. We are not supposed to outlive our children. Rather, we assume that they will have many years to enjoy life after we are gone, and because we have lived a long and full life, there will be many stories for them to tell their children, many memories for them to share with their siblings. When a child dies, the stories end prematurely. The number of years we have lived may be far greater than the number of stories we can relate about their lives. Therefore, we repeat. The only other option is for us to unnaturally limit our conversations, stop including our children in our holiday celebrations, and restrict them to our personal memories. In my opinion, doing so diminishes their value, both to us and to others who loved them.

I choose to continually take the risk and not diminish my son's memory. He brought much joy to my life, the least I can do is insist that his spirit remain alive as long as I am here on this earth. That is my ultimate goal in this writing. Michael was a complex, charming, and troubled young man who made a difference in my life and in the lives of many others. My effort is worth it; he deserves no less.

So I will continue to repeat "Michael stories." I will relate examples of his antics growing up, I will remind others of the humor he displayed, and I will retell aspects of the struggle he experienced. When those to whom I speak indicate boredom or some other negative reaction, they will fall into one of two groups: people who matter to me and people who do not. The latter I can live without. For those who continue to have a place in my life, I will ask them to be patient with me. I will urge them to understand that my repetitious stories are necessary, and I will love them for laughing anyway, for not being afraid of my tears, and perhaps for being willing to cry with me.

I urge all bereaved parents to do the same. Take the risk to be honest with those you love. Tell them how you yearn to speak of your child, ask them to allow you to grieve.

16
Hope for the Future

When you are sorrowful look again in your heart, and you shall see that in truth you are weeping for that which has been your delight.

—Kahlil Gibran

Early on in this process of grief, I was not sure there was a future for me. Even now, several years later, there are times when the future seems too dim to enjoy. Time moves on with or without us, and somewhere along the way, you wake up and realize that the future is here. For me, the real question is what will I do with it? Will I allow my sadness to control my tomorrow? How has his death changed me? Who am I becoming, and will I like that person once I get there?

I spent many years of my life just trying to get to know myself; I mean really know myself. It was often a painful process to look honestly at my strengths and weaknesses. Eventually, I made it to a place where I was comfortable enough with myself to relax and enjoy the life around me. There were things I didn't much like about myself, parts of me I continued to try to improve, but overall, I was okay. I learned to rely on my strengths and was less likely to hide from my faults.

Even now, many of the feelings I continue to experience through this grief are foreign to me. The intensity is still frightening at times, almost paralyzing. Life as I knew it, as I planned it, is over, yet I continue to breathe. What will tomorrow look like, and do I really want to be a part of it? Can I find the courage to start over again, allowing myself to become someone new? Is a mother still a mother after she has lost her child? Questions like these continue to invade my thoughts as I go about my daily life. One day leads to the next, and then months and even years pass. Yet a funny thing seems to be happening along the way. As I ponder these questions, the courage and stamina I need to survive becomes a part of me. I can almost feel the strength growing inside of me. This, I believe, is the gift of faith. God does love me, and He loves my son. Just as Michael is now in His arms, I too am surrounded by His love. I will go on, not just because I have no choice, but because there is a purpose to my life, too. I am not always aware of exactly what that purpose is, but I know in my heart that it is not over.

Perhaps a part of that purpose lies within this writing. In the introduction, I indicated that at least in part, my purpose in this effort is a selfish one, an integral part of my healing. It has taken several years to complete this task, and in that time, I have learned a great deal about myself and the process of grief.

So where do we go from here? The sum and substance of successfully moving through the process of grief is just that—moving through. It is senseless to try to control it. Just let it happen. Be what and who you are in the moment and know that the moment too will pass. Accept the fact that you are becoming a different person without your child and believe that you will be better, not worse. Would your child have it any other way?

I am different since Michael died, and as the days pass I am beginning to like the woman I am becoming. I don't care so much about what others think of me anymore, because I am the one living in my skin, after all. I'm not as intimidated by people who are obviously smarter than I. What difference does more intelligence really make? I don't look at life nearly as seriously as I once did, because I know from experience that it can be gone in a fraction of a second. So why not enjoy life while it's here and help others to do the same?

Experiencing a devastating loss like the death of my only child has put things into perspective for me. Most of what once mattered does not much matter anymore, and what does matter is now very clear. The change of seasons matters, feeling the sun on my face matters, the beauty and scent of flowers matter, and my family and friends, especially those who have been with me through it all, matter. Being able to laugh again matters more than ever, and crying without shame matters too. I have learned to enjoy my own company and have the presence of mind to realize what a gift that is. I have learned to allow others to care for me because I no longer always need to be in control. I recognize that it's not the length of my life that matters, but what I do with it while I am here. My son's death has taught me to cherish each day as an opportunity to become more, to enjoy more, to understand more, and to reach out more.

Michael was a complex child, a rebellious teenager, and a complicated young man. He had much to learn about life, love, and himself. He only lived for twenty-six years, so I guess it's no surprise he still had a lot to learn. What may come as a surprise, though, is how much he had to teach those who knew him. He taught me to be more patient. He taught me the healing power of laughter. He taught me the value of family and friends. My son died on May 7, 2003. Life as I knew it ended that day, but because of my faith, I knew that a new life would someday begin. It has. I have felt Michael's spirit many times since that day. I know he is still with me in ways I don't always understand. He is still teaching me.

Since Michael's death, my greatest fear has always been that someday he will be forgotten. Perhaps that is in fact the greater purpose in this writing. The words on these pages will last long after I'm gone, and as such, his spirit will live on. He became a part of me the moment I first held him in my arms, and nothing has ever changed that fact. Keeping his spirit alive allows me to continue to breathe, to laugh, and to love. I owe a great deal to my son, so I continue to enjoy the life I have even though he is not physically with me. He is present in my heart, and now he is present in my words.

He is also present in the various "memorials" that have been established in his name. Previously I mentioned the memorial tree donated by loving friends and planted in a park near my home. I love that tree and the beautiful area surrounding it. I go there often to be with Michael. I bring a book, sometimes a sandwich, and I sit and read while I have lunch with my son. I realize that saying such things may sound silly to some, but that's another thing I have learned in this process. What may appear silly or even eccentric to others often brings comfort and solace to me. So what's the harm? I encourage bereaved parents to risk sounding silly if it brings a sense of peace and warmth to your heart.

I visited Michael's tree on the first anniversary of his death. When I arrived, I was pleasantly surprised to see that someone had planted flowers around the base of the tree. At the time, I had no idea where this "gift" came from. Looking around, I could not help but notice that no such beauty rested at the foot of the other memorial trees in the park. This "gift" was obviously personal, and I felt the love and support it conveyed. Several days later, I mentioned the flowers to my sister-in-law, and I could tell by her slight smile that she had been the one who offered this "gift." In the midst of her workday, she had traveled several miles to the park, lovingly planted the colorful flowers, and returned to work, saying nothing to me about her journey. That kind of loving expression of support remains with you for years. Julie touched my heart that day through planting those flowers, caring enough to make the effort and never asking even for my gratitude in return. What a gift!

I have a number of other memorials throughout my home. There is a digital frame that I turn on occasionally and watch the pictures of Michael scan through the years of his life. There is a DVD I now have of family pictures with memories attached, memories that include the speech he gave at my retirement party. There is the tribute that hangs in my front entry, greeting everyone who steps into my home. It's a large picture of Michael standing next to a seven-foot tall bottle of Tabasco sauce. The picture was taken by his friends when they traveled to Louisiana several years ago. Below the picture is a small plaque on which hang two of Michael's favorite possessions: his black leather jacket and his blue Chicago Cubs baseball cap. All of these reminders will remain in my home because it will always be his home too.

Finally, I researched and found a wonderful organization in a nearby town that helped me establish a permanent memorial in the form of a scholarship. I started it about three years after he died. I am not wealthy, and the scholarship amount is nowhere near the cost of a year of college these days. Yet it is my sincere hope that even the small amount I can afford will help other young people develop their talents through higher education. As of this writing, there have been three recipients of the Michael David McGrath Scholarship Fund, and I hope that many more will follow. I find it just another way to keep his spirit alive, and I am committed to continuing it as long as I can.

All of these examples add a positive dimension to my life without my son. I wholeheartedly encourage other bereaved parents to discover ways to memorialize their children. Such efforts can help to fill the void that is created by their death.

I hope the previous pages have introduced you to my son, Michael. He was an extraordinary and complex young man with many gifts and more personal struggles than seemed fair. I feel it's important for you to know him, at least a little, in order to understand the pain I live with every day after losing him. Perhaps if you understand him, it will help you understand the depth of my grief.

So my choice is to live and cherish each day on this earth. That is what my son would want for me, and I will not disappoint him. He was the joy of my life while on this earth, and now his joy once again fills my heart. There are days when I long to see his smile again, to hear his voice and his laughter, and my faith is strong enough to know that day will come. In the meantime, I miss him dearly. I will always miss him *just every day.*